March of America Facsimile Series

Number 50

The Discovery and
Settlement of Kentucke

John Filson

The Discovery and Settlement of Kentucke

by John Filson

ANN ARBOR

UNIVERSITY MICROFILMS, INC.

A Subsidiary of Xerox Corporation

Foreword

John Filson's *The Discovery, Settlement And present State of Kentucke: ... To which is added, An Appendix, Containing, The Adventures of Col. Daniel Boon...*, published at Wilmington, Delaware, in 1784, is the first descriptive account of Kentucky and the first narrative of Daniel Boone. Filson's work was immediately popular and has been many times reprinted. It was translated into French and a Paris edition appeared in 1785. It was also reprinted in London. Although Filson claimed that he was reprinting Boone's own story, which he relates in the first person, it is clear from the high flown style that Filson himself is the author. The poet Byron evidently read Filson and obtained from him material on Boone which he wove into *Don Juan*.

Filson's historical material is sometimes incorrect and misleading, but the descriptive portions of his account are more accurate, and the map which he had printed separately in Philadelphia was the best up to that time for the topography of the Kentucky country. It was widely used for many years.

Little is known about Filson's early career except that he came from Pennsylvania and apparently went to Kentucky to take up lands awarded by Virginia to war veterans. For a time he seems to have taught school at Lexington. After a trip back to Pennsylvania, he returned to Kentucky and lived for a while at Louisville where he was a fur trader. In 1788, he published in the *Kentucky Gazette* a prospectus of a school that he proposed to set up in Lexington, and later in the same year, a prospectus for a town in Ohio which he and associates proposed to establish. In October 1788, while surveying a tract of land on the Little Miami River he was shot and killed by an Indian.

Filson's *Discovery* is a fascinating document with vivid pictures of the country that must have excited the interest of many prospective emigrants. Filson comments in his preface that at the time of publication he was "not an inhabitant of Kentucke, but having been there some time by my acquaintance in it, am sufficiently able to publish the truth, and from principle have cautiously endeavoured to avoid every species of falsehood." Certainly his contemporaries took his description at face value, and the book had an influence on the development of the West. Filson had the wisdom to see that control of the Mississippi River was essential to the future prosperity of the country. He took a cynical view of the treaty with Spain guaranteeing unmolested navigation of the great river, for, he says, "experience teaches mankind that treaties are not always to be depended on, the most solemn being broken. Hence we learn that no one should put much faith in any state; and the trade and commerce of the Mississippi River cannot be so well secured in any other possession as our own."

In "The Adventures of Col. Daniel Boon," which Filson puts into Boone's own mouth, he relates a succession of encounters with the Indians in which many hunters and settlers meet their deaths. Boone loses two sons and a brother and narrowly escapes with his own life. This tale helped to establish the legend of Daniel Boone as a frontier hero.

A brief account of Filson will be found in the *Dictionary of American Biography.* W. R. Jillson in *Filson's Kentucke, a Facsimile Reproduction of the Original Wilmington Edition of 1784* (Louisville, Ky., 1929) gives a life of Filson and a bibliography of his work.

THE
DISCOVERY, SETTLEMENT

And present State of

K E N T U C K E:

A N D

An ESSAY towards the TOPOGRAPHY, and NATURAL HISTORY of that important Country:

To which is added,

An A P P E N D I X,

C O N T A I N I N G,

I. The ADVENTURES of Col. *Daniel Boon*, one of the firſt Settlers, comprehending every important Occurrence in the political Hiſtory of that Province.

II The MINUTES of the *Piankaſhaw* council, held at *Poſt St. Vincents, April* 15, 1784.

III. An ACCOUNT of the *Indian* Nations inhabiting within the Limits of the Thirteen United States, their Manners and Cuſtoms, and Reflections on their Origin.

IV. The STAGES and DISTANCES between *Philadelphia* and the Falls of the *Ohio;* from *Pittſburg* to *Penſacola* and ſeveral other Places. —The Whole illuſtrated by a new and accurate MAP of *Kentucke* and the Country adjoining, drawn from actual Surveys.

By *J O H N F I L S O N.*

Wilmington, Printed by JAMES ADAMS, 1784.

WE the Subscribers, inhabitants of Kentucke, and well acquainted with the country from its first settlement, at the request of the author of this book, and map, have carefully revised them, and recommend them to the public, as exceeding good performances, containing as accurate a description of our country as we think can possibly be given; much preferable to any in our knowledge extant; and think it will be of great utility to the publick. Witness our hands this 12th day of May, Anno Domini 1784,

DANIEL BOON,
LEVI TODD,
JAMES HARROD.

PREFACE.

THE generality of those geographers, who have attempted a map, or description of A-merica, seem either to have had no knowledge of Kentucke, or to have neglected it, although a place of infinite importance: And the rest have proceeded so erroneously, that they have left the world as much in darkness as before. Many are the mistakes, re-specting the subject of this work, in all other maps which I have yet seen; whereas I can truly say, I know of none in that which I here present to the world either from my own particular knowledge, or from the information of those gentlemen with whose assistance I have been favoured, and who have been well acquainted with the country since the first settle-ment. When I visited Kentucke, I found it so far to exceed my expectations, although great, that I con-cluded it was a pity, that the world had not adequate information of it. I conceived that a proper descrip-tion, and map of it, were objects highly interesting to the United States; and therefore, incredible as it may appear to some, I must declare, that this perform-ance is not published from lucrative motives, but solely to inform the world of the happy climate, and

plentiful

plentiful soil of this favoured region. And I ima-
gine the reader will believe me the more easily when I
inform him, that I am not an inhabitant of Kentuc-
ke, but having been there some time, by my acquain-
tance in it, am sufficiently able to publish the truth,
and from principle, have cautiously endeavoured to
avoid every species of falsehood. The consciousness of
this encourages me to hope for the public candour,
where errors may possibly be found. The three
gentlemen honouring this work with their recommen-
dation, Col Boon, Col. Todd, and Col. Harrod, were
among the first settlers, and perfectly well acquaint-
ed with the country. To them I acknowledge myself
much indebted for their friendly assistance in this work,
which they chearfully contributed with a difinterested
view of being serviceable to the public. My thanks
are more especially due to Col. Boon, who was earli-
er acquainted with the subject of this performance
than any other now living, as appears by the ac-
count of his adventures, which I esteemed curious
and interesting, and therefore have published them
from his own mouth. Much advantage may possi-
bly arise to the possessor of this book, as those who
wish to travel in Kentucke will undoubtedly find it
a Compleat Guide. To such I affirm, that there is
nothing mentioned or described but what they will
find true. Conscious that it would be of general utility,
I have omitted nothing, and been exceeding particu-
lar in every part. That it may have the desired
effect, is the sincere wish of

JOHN FILSON.

THE

DISCOVERY, PURCHASE

AND

SETTLEMENT,

OF

KENTUCKE.

THE firſt white man we have certain accounts of, who diſcovered this province,
was one James M‘Bride, who, in company with
ſome others, in the year 1754, paſſing down the
Ohio in Canoes, landed at the mouth of Kentucke river, and there marked a tree, with the
firſt letters of his name, and the date, which
remain to this day. Theſe men reconnoitred
the country, and returned home with the pleaſ-
ing news of their diſcovery of the beſt tract of
land in North-America, and probably in the
world.

wórld. From this period it remained concealed till about the year 1767, when one John Finley, and fome others, trading with the Indians, fortunately travelled over the fertile region, now called Kentucke, then but known to the Indians, by the name of the Dark and Bloody Ground, and fometimes the Middle Ground. This country greatly engaged Mr. Finley's attention. Some time after, difputes arifing between the Indians and traders, he was obliged to decamp; and returned to his place of refidence in North-Carolina, where he communicated his difcovery to Col. Daniel Boon, and a few more, who conceiving it to be an interefting object, agreed in the year 1769 to undertake a journey in order to explore it. After a long fatiguing march, over a mountainous wildernefs, in a weftward direction, they at length arrived upon its borders; and from the top of an eminence, with joy and wonder, defcried the beautiful landfcape of Kentucke. Here they encamped, and fome went to hunt provifions, which were readily procured, there being plenty of game, while Col. Boon and John Finley made a tour through the country, which they found far exceeding their expectations, and returning to camp, informed their companions of their difcoveries: But in fpite of this promifing beginning, this company, meeting with nothing but hardfhips and adver-

fity,

fity, grew exceedingly difheartened, and was plundered, difperfed, 'and killed by the Indians, except Col. Boon, who continued an inhabitant of the wildernefs until the year 1771, when he returned home.

About this time Kentucke had drawn the attention of feveral gentlemen. Doctor Walker of Virginia, with a number more, made a tour weftward for difcoveries, endeavouring to find the Ohio river; and afterwards he and General Lewis, at Fort Stanwix, purchafed from the Five Nations of Indians the lands lying on the north fide of Kentucke. Col. Donaldfon, of Virginia, being employed by the State to run a line from fix miles above the Long Ifland, on Holftein, to the mouth of the great Kenhawa, and finding thereby that an extenfive tract of excellent country would be cut off to the Indians, was folicited, by the inhabitants of Clench and Holftein, to purchafe the lands lying on the north fide of Kentucke river from the Five Nations. This purchafe he compleated for five hundred pounds, fpecie. It was then agreed, to fix a boundary line, running from the long Ifland on Holftein to the head of Kentucke river: thence down the fame to the mouth; thence up the Ohio, to the mouth of Great Kenhawa; but this valuable purchafe the State refufed to confirm.

B

Col.

Col. Henderſon, of North-Carolina, being informed of this country by Col. Boon, he, and ſome other gentlemen, held a treaty with the Cherokee Indians at Wataga, in March 1775, and then purchaſed from them the lands lying on the ſouth ſide of Kentucke river for goods, at valuable rates, to the amount of ſix thouſand pounds, ſpecie.

Soon after this purchaſe, the State of Virginia took the alarm, agreed to pay the money Col. Donaldſon had contracted for, and then diſputed Col. Henderſon's right of purchaſe, as a private gentlemen of another ſtate, in behalf of himſelf : However, for his eminent ſervices to this country, and for having been inſtrumental in making ſo valuable an acquiſition to Virginia, that ſtate was pleaſed to reward him with a tract of land, at the mouth of Green River, to the amount of two hundred thouſand acres ; and the ſtate of North-Carolina gave him the like quantity in Powel's Valley. This region was formerly claimed by various tribes of Indians ; whoſe title, if they had any, originated in ſuch a manner, as to render it doubtful which ought to poſſeſs it : Hence this fertile ſpot became an object of contention, a theatre of war, from which it was properly denominated the Bloody-Grounds. Their contentions not being likely to decide the Right to any particular tribe, as

ſoon

foon as Mr. Henderſon and his friends propoſed to purchaſe, the Indians agreed to ſell; and notwithſtanding the valuable Conſideration they received, have continued ever ſince troubleſome neighbours to the new ſettlers.

SITUATION and BOUNDARIES.

KENTUCKE is ſituated, in its central part, near the latitude of 38 °½ north, and 85° weſt longitude, and lying within the fifth climate, its longeſt day is 14 hours 40 minutes. It is bounded on the north by great Sandy-creek; by the Ohio on the N. W. by North-Carolina on the ſouth; and by the Cumberland mountain on the eaſt, being upwards of 250 miles in length, and two hundred in breadth; and is at preſent divided into three counties, Lincoln, Fayette and Jefferſon; of which Fayette and Jefferſon are bounded by the Ohio, and the river Kentucke ſeparates Fayette on its north ſide from the other two. There are at preſent eight towns laid off, and building; and more are propoſed.

Louiſville, at the Falls of Ohio, and Beardstown, are in Jefferſon county; Harrodſburg, Danville, and Boons-burrow, in Lincoln county; Lexington, Lees-town, and Greenville, in Fayette county; the two laſt being on Kentucke river. At theſe and many other places, on
this

this and other rivers, infpecting-houfes are eftablifhed for Tobacco, which may be cultivated to great advantage; although not altogether the ftaple commodity of the country.

R I V E R S.

THE beautiful river Ohio, bounds Kentucke in its whole length, being a mile and fometimes lefs in breadth, and is fufficient to carry boats of great burthen. Its general courfe is fouth 60 degrees weft; and in its courfe it receives numbers of large and fmall rivers, which pay tribute to its glory. The only difadvantage this fine river has, is a rapid, one mile and an half long, and one mile and a quarter broad, called the Falls of Ohio. In this place the river runs over a rocky bottom, and the defcent is fo gradual, that the fall does not probably in the whole exceed twenty feet. In fome places we may obferve it to fall a few feet. When the ftream is low, empty boats only can pafs and repafs this rapid; their lading muft be tranfported by land; but when high, boats of any burthen may pafs in fafety. Excepting this place, there is not a finer river in the world for navigation by boats. Befides this, Kentucke is watered by eight fmaller rivers, and many large and fmall creeks, as may be eafily feen in the map.

Licking

Licking River heading in the mountains with Cumberland River, and the North Branch of Kentucke, runs in a N. W. direction for upwards of a hundred miles, collecting its silver ftreams from many branches, and is about one hundred yards broad at its mouth.

Red River heads and interlocks with the main branch of Licking, and flows in a S. Weft courfe into Kentucke River, being about fixty miles long, and fixty yards wide at its mouth.

The Kentucke River rifes with three heads from a mountainous part of the Country. Its northern branch interlocks with Cumberland; runs half way in a weftern direction, and the other half N. wefterly. It is amazingly crooked, upwards of two hundred miles in length, and about one hundred and fifty yards broad.

Elkhorn is a fmall river which empties itfelf into Kentucke in a N. W. by W. courfe; is about fifty miles long, and fifty yards broad at the mouth.

Dick's River joins the Kentucke in a N. Weft direction; is about forty-five miles long, and forty-five yards wide at its mouth. This river curioufly heads and interlocks its branches with Salt River, Green River, and the waters
of

of Rock-caftle River.—Salt River rifes at four different places near each other. The windings of this river are curious, rolling its ftreams round a fpacious tract of fine land, and uniting almoft fifteen miles before they approach the Ohio, and twenty miles below the Falls. It is amazingly crooked, runs a weftern courfe near ninety miles, and is about eighty yards wide at the mouth.

Green River interlocking with the heads of Dick's River, as mentioned above, is alfo a-mazingly crooked, keeps a weftern courfe for upwards of one hundred and fifty miles, and is about eighty yards wide at its mouth, which is about two hundred and twenty miles below the Falls.

Cumberland River, interlocks with the north-ern branch of Kentucke, as aforefaid, and rol-ling round the other arms of Kentucke, among the mountains, in a fouthern courfe for one hundred miles; then in a fouth weftern courfe for above one hundred miles; then in a fouth-ern and S. weftern courfe for about two hun-dred and fifty more, finds the Ohio, four hun-dred and thirteen miles below the Falls. At the fettlements it is two hundred yards broad; and at its mouth three hundred, having paffed

fed through North-Carolina in about half its courfe.

The Great Kenhawa, or New River, rifes in North-Carolina, runs a northern, and N. Weft courfe for upwards of four hundred miles, and finds the Ohio four hundred miles above the Falls. It is about five hundred yards wide at its mouth. Thefe two rivers are juft mentioned, being beyond our limits. They run contrary courfes, are exceeding large, and it is worth notice, that Clench, Holftein, Nolachuckey, and French-Broad rivers, take their rife between thefe two, or rather weftward of New River, fome of them rifing and interlocking with it; and when they meet, form what is called the Tenefe, or Cherokee River, which runs a weftern courfe, and finds the Ohio twelve miles below Cumberland River. It is very large, and has fpacious tracts of fine land.

Thefe rivers are navigable for boats almoft to their fources, without rapids, for the greateft part of the year. This country is generally level, and abounding with limeftone, which ufually lies about fix feet deep, except in hollows, where ftreams run, where we find the rock in the bottom of the channel.

The fprings and ftreams leffen in June, and
continue

continue low, hindering navigation, until November, when the autumnal rains foon pre-
pare the rivers for boats, and replenifh the
whole country with water; but although the
ftreams decreafe, yet there is always fufficient
for domeftic ufes. There are many fine fprings,
that never fail; every farmer has a good one at
leaft; and excellent wells may eafily be dug.

Nature of the SOIL.

THE country, in fome parts, is nearly level;
in others not fo much fo; in others again hilly,
but moderately, and in fuch places there is
moft water. The levels are not like a carpet,
but interfperfed with fmall rifings, and declivi-
ties, which form a beautiful profpect. A great
part of the foil is amazingly fertile; fome not
fo good, and fome poor. The inhabitants diftinguifh its quality by firft, fecond, and third
rate lands; and fcarcely any fuch thing as a
marfh or fwamp is to be found. There is a
ridge, where Kentucke rifes, nearly of the fize
of a mountain, which in the map we have
reprefented as fuch.

All the land below the Great Kenhawa until we come near the waters of Licking River
is broken, hilly, and generally poor; except
in fome valleys, and on Little and Big Sandy
creeks

creeks, where there is fome firft rate land, but moftly fecond and third rate. It is faid, that near this water is found a pure falt rock. Upon the north branch of Licking, we find a great body of firft rate land. This ftream runs nearly parallel to the Ohio for a confiderable diftance, and is about feven miles from the mouth of Limeftone Creek, where is a fine harbour for boats coming down the Ohio, and now a common landing. It is fixty-five miles from Lexington, to which there is a large waggon road. The main branch of Licking, is about twenty-two miles from Limeftone. On this ftream we find fome firft, but moftly fecond and third rate lands, and towards its head fomething hilly. There we find the Blue Licks, two fine falt fprings, where great plenty of falt may be made. Round thefe licks, the foil is poor for fome diftance, being much impregnated with falt.

The fouthern branch of Licking, and all its other arms, as appears in the map, fpread through a great body of firft, and fome fecond rate land, where there is abundance of cane, and fome falt licks, and fprings. On thefe feveral branches of Licking, are good mill-feats, and navigation to the Ohio, from the fork down to its mouth. The land is hilly, and generally

C   poor,

poor, yet along the ftreams and in valleys we find fome excellent land.

The Elkhorn lands are much efteemed, being fituated in a bend of Kentucke River, of great extent, in which this little river, or rather large creek, rifes. Here we find moftly firft rate land, and near the Kentucke River fecond and third rate. This great tract is beautifully fitu- ated, covered with cane, wild rye, and clover; and many of the ftreams afford fine mill feats.

The lands below the mouth of Elkhorn, up Eagle Creek, and towards the Ohio, are hilly and poor, except thofe contained in a great bend of the Ohio, oppofite Great Miami, cut off, as appears in the map, by the Big-bone and Bank-lick creeks, interlocking, and run- ning feparate courfes. Here we find a great deal of good land, but fomething hilly.

On Kentucke River we find many fertile valleys, or bottoms along the river, efpecially towards its rife. There is good land alfo on Red River, but towards the heads of this, and Kentucke, the foil is broken; but even here, we find in valleys, and along ftreams, a great deal of fruitful land. Generally the foil within a mile or two of Kentucke River is of the third
and

and fourth rates; from about that diſtance, as
we leave it on either ſide, we approach good
lands. The country through which it winds its
courſe, for the moſt part, may be conſidered as
level to its banks, or rather precipices; from the
brow of which, we behold the river, three and
ſometimes four hundred feet deep, like a great
canal. For a more particular account of this,
we refer the reader to where we treat of the cu‑
rioſities of Kentucke.

Dick's River runs through a great body of
firſt rate land, abounding every where with
cane, and affords many excellent mill ſeats.
Many mills are already built on this ſtream,
ſome of which are repreſented in the map, and
will have a plentiful ſupply of water in the dry‑
eſt ſeaſons. The banks of this river, near its
mouth, are ſimilar to the banks of Kentucke.
The ſeveral ſtreams and branches of Salt River
afford excellent mill ſeats. Theſe roll them‑
ſelves through a great tract of excellent land,
but the country from the junction of theſe
waters, and ſome miles above towards the Ohio,
which may be about twenty-five miles, is level
and poor, and has abundance of ponds. For a
conſiderable diſtance from the head of this
river, the land is of the firſt quality, well ſitu‑
ated, and abounds with fine cane. Upon this,
and

and Dick's River, the inhabitants are chiefly fettled, it being the fafeft part of the country from
the incurfions of the Indians.

Green River, affords excellent mill feats, and
a conftant ftream. This is allowed to be the
beft watered part of Kentucke. On its banks we
find many fine bottoms, fome firft rate, but
moftly fecond and third rate lands; and at fome
diftance, many knobs, ridges, and broken poor
land. Below a creek, called Sinking Creek, on
this river, within fifty miles of Ohio, towards
Salt River, a great territory begins, called
Green River Barrens, extending to the Ohio.
Moft of this is very good land, and level. It
has no timber, and little water, but affords
excellent pafturage for cattle. On fome parts
of this river, we find abundance of cane, fome
falt licks, and fulphureous and bituminous
fprings. South of Green River, in the lands
referved for the continental, and ftate troops of
Virginia, an exceeding valuable lead mine has
lately been difcovered. Iron ore is found on
Rough Creek, a ftream running into this river.
That part of Cumberland River which is in the
Kentucke country, traverfes a hilly poor land,
though in fome parts we find good foil along its
fides. The other rivers I mentioned (viz. Great
Kenhawa, and Tenefe) are not in the Kentucke
country, and therefore do not come properly
within my plan. The

The reader, by cafting his eye upon the map, and viewing round the heads of Licking, from the Ohio, and round the heads of Kentucke, Dick's River, and down Green River to the Ohio, may view, in that great compafs of above one hundred miles fquare, the moft extraordinary country that the fun enlightens with his celeftial beams.

The Ohio River, the great refervoir of all the numerous rivers that flow into it from both fides, has many fine valleys along its fides; and we obferve that oppofite to each of them there is a hill; thefe hills and bottoms changing fides alternately. It only remains under this head to inform the reader, that there is a great body of firft rate land near the Falls, or Rapids, called Bare-grafs; and it will be fufficient juft to mention that the country on the N. Weft fide of the Ohio, fome of the waters of which I have reprefented in the map, is allowed by all travellers to be a moft fertile, level country, and well watered.

AIR AND CLIMATE.

THIS country is more temperate and healthy than the other fettled parts of America. In Summer it wants the fandy heats which Virginia and Carolina experience, and receives a fine air

from

from its rivers. In Winter, which at moſt only laſts three months, commonly two, and is but ſeldom ſevere, the people are ſafe in bad houſes; and the beaſts have a good ſupply without fodder. The Winter begins about Chriſtmas, and ends about the firſt of March, at fartheſt does not exceed the middle of that month. Snow ſeldom falls deep or lies long. The weſt winds often bring ſtorms, and the eaſt winds clear the ſky; but there is no ſteady rule of weather in that reſpect as in the northern ſtates. The weſt winds are ſometimes cold and nitrous. The Ohio running in that direction, and there being mountains on that quarter, the weſterly winds by ſweeping along their tops, in the cold regions of the air, and over a long tract of frozen water, collect cold in their courſe, and convey it over the Kentucke country; but the weather is not ſo intenſely ſevere as theſe winds bring with them in Pennſylvania. The air and ſeaſons depend very much on the winds, as to heat and cold, dryneſs and moiſture.

SOIL AND PRODUCE.

THE ſoil of Kentucke is of a looſe, deep black mould, without ſand, in the firſt rate lands about two or three feet deep, and exceeding luxurious in all its productions. In ſome places the mould inclines to brown. In ſome the wood, as

the

the natural confequence of too rich a foil, is of
little value, appearing like dead timber and large
ftumps in a field lately cleared. Thefe parts are
not confiderable. The country in general may be
confidered as well timbered, producing large trees
of many kinds, and to be exceeded by no country
in variety. Thofe which are peculiar to Kentucke
are the fugar-tree, which grows in all parts in great
plenty, and furnifhes every family with plenty of
excellent fugar. The honey-locuft is curioufly
furrounded with large thorny fpikes, bearing
broad and long pods in form of peas, has a
fweet tafte, and makes excellent beer.

The coffee-tree greatly refembles the black
oak, grows large, and alfo bears a pod, in which
is enclofed good coffee. The pappa-tree does
not grow to a great fize, is a foft wood, bears
a fine fruit much like a cucumber in fhape and
fize, and taftes fweet. The cucumber-tree is
fmall and foft, with remarkable leaves, bears a
fruit much refembling that from which it is nam-
ed. Black mulberry-trees are in abundance. The
wild cherry-tree is here frequent, of a large fize,
and fupplies the inhabitants with boards for all
their buildings. Here alfo is the buck-eye, an
exceeding foft wood, bearing a remarkable black
fruit, and fome other kinds of trees not common
elfewhere. Here is great plenty of fine cane, on
which the cattle feed, and grow fat. This plant
in

in general grows from three to twelve feet high, of
a hard fubftance, with joints at eight or ten inches
diftance along the ftalk, from which proceed leaves
refembling thofe of the willow. There are many
cane brakes fo thick and tall that it is difficult to pafs
through them. Where no cane grows there is a-
bundance of wild-rye, clover, and buffalo-grafs,
covering vaft tracts of country, and affording excellent food for cattle. The fields are covered
with abundance of wild herbage not common to
other countries. The Shawanefe fallad, wild let-
tuce, and pepper-grafs, and many more, as yet
unknown to the inhabitants, but which, no
doubt, have excellent virtues. Here are feen
the fineft crown-imperial in the world, the car-
dinal flower, fo much extolled for its fcarlet colour; and all the year, excepting the three Winter
months, the plains and valleys are adorned with
variety of flowers of the moft admirable beauty.
Here is alfo found the tulip-bearing laurel-tree, or
magnolia, which has an exquifite fmell, and con-
tinues to bloffom and feed for feveral months
together.

This country is richeft on the higher lands,
exceeding the fineft low grounds in the fettled
parts of the continent. When cultivated it pro-
duces in common fifty and fixty bufhels per a-
cre; and I have heard it affirmed by credible
perfons, that above one hundred bufhels of good
corn

corn were produced from an acre in one feafon.
The firft rate land is too rich for wheat till it has
been reduced by four or five years cultivation.

Col. Harrod, a gentleman of veracity in Kentucke, has lately experienced the production of
fmall grain, and affirms, that he had thirty-five
bufhels of wheat, and fifty bufhels of rye per a-
cre.

I think in common the land will produce a-
bout thirty bufhels of wheat, and rye, upon a
moderate computation, per acre; and this is the
general opinion of the inhabitants. We may
fuppofe that barley and oats will increafe abundantly; as yet they have not been fufficiently
tried. The foil is very favourable to flax and
hemp, turnips, potatoes and cotton, which
grow in abundance; and the fecond, third and
fourth rate lands, are as proper for fmall grain.
Thefe accounts of fuch amazing fertility may,
to fome, appear incredible, but are certainly
true. Every hufbandman may have a good gar-
den, or meadow, without water or manure,
where he pleafes. The foil, which is not of a thir-
fty nature, is commonly well fupplied with plentiful fhowers.

Iron ore and lead are found in abundance, but we
do not hear of any filver or gold mine as yet difcovered.   D   The

The weſtern waters produce plenty of fiſh and fowl. The fiſh common to the waters of the Ohio are the buffalo-fiſh, of a large ſize, and the cat-fiſh ſometimes exceeding one hundred weight. Salmons have been taken in Kentucke weighing thirty weight. The mullet, rock, perch, gar-fiſh, and eel, are here in plenty. It is ſaid that there are no trouts in the weſtern waters. Suckers, ſun-fiſh, and other hook-fiſh, are abundant ; but no ſhad, or herrings. We may ſuppoſe with a degree of certainty, that there are large ſubterraneous aqueducts ſtored with fiſh,. from whence fine ſprings ariſe in many parts producing fine hook-fiſh in variety. On theſe waters, and eſpecially on the Ohio, the geeſe and ducks are amazingly numerous.

The land fowls are turkeys, which are very frequent, pheaſants, partridges, and ravens : The perraquet, a bird every way reſembling a parrot, but much ſmaller ; the ivory-bill wood-cock, of a whitiſh colour with a white plume, flies ſcreaming exceeding ſharp. It is aſſerted, that the bill of this bird is pure ivory, a circumſtance very ſingular in the plumy tribe. The great owl reſembles its ſpecies in other parts, but is remarkably different in its vociferation, ſometimes making a ſtrange, ſurpriſing noiſe, like a man in the moſt extreme danger and difficulty.

Serpents

Serpents are not numerous, and are fuch as are to be found in other parts of the continent, except the bull, the horned and the mockafon fnakes. Swamps are rare, and confequently frogs and other reptiles, common to fuch places. There are no fwarms of bees, except fuch as have been introduced by the prefent inhabitants.

QUADRUPEDS.

AMONG the native animals are the urus, or zorax, defcribed by Cefar, which we call a buffalo, much refembling a large bull, of a great fize, with a large head, thick fhort crooked horns, and broader in his forepart than behind. Upon his fhoulder is a large lump of flefh, covered with a thick bofs of long wool and curly hair, of a dark brown colour. They do not rife from the ground as our cattle, but fpring up at once upon their feet; are of a broad make and clumfy appearance, with fhort legs, but run faft, and turn not afide for any thing when chafed, except a ftanding tree. They weigh from five to ten hundred weight, are excellent meat, fupplying the inhabitants in many parts with beef, and their hides make good leather. I have heard a hunter affert, he faw above one thoufand buffaloes at the Blue Licks at once; fo numerous were they before the firft fettlers had wantonly fported away their lives. There ftill remains

mains a great number in the exterior parts of the settlement. They feed upon cane and grass, as other cattle, and are innocent harmlefs creatures.

There are still to be found many deer, elks and bears, within the settlement, and many more on the borders of it. There are also panthers, wild-cats, and wolves.

The waters have plenty of beavers, otters, minks, and musk-rats : Nor are the animals common to other parts wanting, such as foxes, rabbits, squirrels, racoons, ground-hogs, pole-cats, and oppossums. Most of the species of the domestic quadrupeds have been introduced since the settlement, such as horses, cows, sheep and hogs, which are prodigiously multiplied, suffered to run in the woods without a keeper, and only brought home when wanted.

INHABITANTS.

AN accurate account is kept of all the male inhabitants above the age of sixteen, who are rated towards the expences of the government by the name of Tithables ; from which, by allowing that those so enrolled amount to a fourth part of the whole inhabitants, we may conclude that Kentucke contains, at present, upwards of thirty
thousand

thousand souls : So amazingly rapid has been the settlement in a few years. Numbers are daily arriving, and multitudes expected this Fall; which gives a well grounded expectation that the country will be exceedingly populous in a short time. The inhabitants, at present, have not extraordinary good houses, as usual in a newly settled country.

They are, in general, polite, humane, hospitable, and very complaisant. Being collected from different parts of the continent, they have a diversity of manners, customs and religions, which may in time perhaps be modified to one uniform. As yet united to the State of Virginia, they are governed by her wholesome laws, which are virtuously executed, and with excellent decorum. Schools for education are formed, and a college is appointed by act of Assembly of Virginia, to be founded under the conduct of trustees in Kentucke, and endowed with lands for its use. An excellent library is likewise bestowed upon this seminary, by the Rev. John Todd, of Virginia.

The Anabaptists were the first that promoted public worship in Kentucke; and the Presbyterians have formed three large congregations near Harrod's station, and have engaged the Rev. David Rice, of Virginia, to be their pastor. At

Lexington

Lexington, 35 miles from thefe, they have formed another large congregation, and invited the
Rev. Mr. Rankin, of Virginia, to undertake that
charge among them. At prefent there are no other
religious focieties formed, although feveral other
fects have numerous adherents. But from thefe
early movements it is hoped that Kentucke will
eminently fhine in learning and piety, which will
fulfil the wifh of every virtuous citizen.

CURIOSITIES.

AMONGST the natural curiofities of this
country, the winding banks, or rather precipices
of Kentucke, and Dick's Rivers, deferve the firft
place. The aftonifhed eye there beholds almoft
every where three or four hundred feet of a fo-
lid perpendicular lime-ftone rock; in fome parts
a fine white marble, either curioufly arched, pil-
lared or blocked up into fine building ftones.
Thefe precipices, as was obferved before, are like
the fides of a deep trench, or canal; the land a-
bove being level, except where creeks fet in, and
crowned with fine groves of red cedar. It is only at particular places that this river can be crofi-
ed, one of which is worthy of admiration; a
great road large enough for waggons made by
buffaloes, floping with an eafy defcent from the
top to the bottom of a very large fteep hill, at
or near the river above Lees-town.

Caves

Caves are found in this country amazingly large ; in fome of which you may travel feveral miles under a fine limeftone rock, fupported by curious arches and pillars : In moft of them runs a ftream of water.

Near the head of Salt River a fubterranean lake or large pond has lately been difcovered. Col. Bowman fays, that he and a companion travelled in one four hours till he luckily came to the mouth again. The fame gentleman mentions another which operates like an air furnace, and contains much fulphur. An adventurer in any of thefe will have a perfect idea of primeval darknefs.

There appear to be great natural ftores of fulphur and falt in this country. A fpring at Boonfburrow conftantly emits fulphureous particles, and near the fame place is a falt fpring. There is another fulphureous fpring upon Four Mile Creek, a third upon Green River, and many others in different places, abounding with that ufeful mineral.

There are three fprings or ponds of bitumen near Green River, which do not form a ftream, but difgorge themfelves into a common refervoir, and when ufed in lamps anfwer all the purpofes of the fineft oil.

There

There are different places abounding with copperas, eafily procured, and in its prefent impure ftate fufficient for the ufe of the inhabitants; and when refined, equal to any in the world.

There is an allum bank on the fouth fide of Cumberland River, fituated at the bottom of a cliff of rocks projecting over it. In its prefent ftate it has the appearance and poffeffes the virtues of that mineral, and when purified is a beautiful allum.

Many fine falt fprings, whofe places appear in the map, conftantly emit water which, being manufactured, affords great quantities of fine falt. At prefent there is but one, called Bullet's Lick, improved, and this affords falt fufficient for all Kentucke, and exports fome to the Illinois. Salt fells at prefent for twenty fhillings per bufhel; but as fome other fprings are beginning to be worked, no doubt that neceffary article will foon be much cheaper. Drenne's-lick, the Bigbone, and the Blue-licks, fend forth ftreams of falt water. The Nob-lick, and many others, do not produce water, but confift of clay mixed with falt particles : To thefe the cattle repair, and reduce high hills rather to valleys than plains. The amazing herds of Buffaloes which refort thither, by their fize and number, fill the traveller with amazement and terror, efpecially when he
beholds

beholds the prodigious roads they have made from all quarters, as if leading to fome populous city; the vaft fpace of land around thefe fprings defolated as if by a ravaging enemy, and hills reduced to plains; for the land near thofe fprings are chiefly hilly. Thefe are truly curiofities, and the eye can fcarcely be fatisfied with admiring them.

A medicinal fpring is found near the Big-bone Lick, which has perfectly cured the itch by once bathing; and experience in time may difcover in it other virtues. There is another of like nature near Drennen's-Lick.

Near Lexington are to be feen curious fepulchres, full of human fkeletons, which are thus fabricated. Firft, on the ground are laid large broad ftones; on thefe were placed the bodies, feparated from each other by broad ftones, covered with others, which ferve as a bafis for the next arrangement of bodies. In this order they are built, without mortar, growing ftill narrower to the height of a man. This method of burying appears to be totally different from that now practifed by the Indians. For our conjectures on this fubject we beg leave to refer to appendix No. 3.—At a falt fpring, near Ohio river, very large bones are found, far furpaffing the fize of any fpecies of animals now in America. The head appears to have been about three

E

feet

feet long, the ribs feven, and the thigh bones a-
bout four ; one of which is repofited in the library in Philadelphia, and faid to weigh feventy-
eight pounds. The tufks are above a foot in
length, the grinders about five inches fquare,
and eight inches long. Thefe bones have equally
excited the amazement of the ignorant, and at-
tracted the attention of the philofopher. Speci-
mens of them have been fent both to France and
England, where they have been examined with the
greateft diligence, and found upon comparifon to
be remains of the fame fpecies of animals that
produced thofe other foffil bones which have been
difcovered in Tartary, Chili, and feveral other
places, both of the old and new continent.
What animal this is, and by what means its ruins are found in regions fo widely different, and
where none fuch exifts at prefent, is a queftion of
more difficult decifion. The ignorant and fuperftitious Tartars attribute them to a creature,
whom they call Maimon, who, they fay, ufually refides at the bottom of the rivers, and of
whom they relate many marvellous ftories ; but
as this is an affertion totally divefted of proof,
and even of probability, it has juftly been reject-
ed by the learned ; and on the other hand it is
certain, that no fuch amphibious quadruped exifts in our American waters. The bones themfelves bear a great refemblance to thofe of the e-
lephant. There is no other terreftrial animal now
known

known large enough to produce them. The tufks with which they are equally furnifhed, equally produce true ivory. Thefe external refemblances have generally made fuperficial obfervers conclude, that they could belong to no other than that prince of quadrupeds ; and when they firft drew the attention of the world, philofophers feem to have fubfcribed to the fame opinion.---- But if fo, whence is it that the whole fpecies has difappeared from America? An animal fo laborious and fo docile, that the induftry of the Peruvians, which reduced to fervitude and fubjected to education fpecies fo vaftly inferior in thofe qualities, as the Llama and the Paca, could never have overlooked the elephant, if he had been to be found in their country. Whence is it that thefe bones are found in climates where the elephant, a native of the torrid zone, cannot even fubfift in his wild ftate, and in a ftate of fervitude will not propagate ? Thefe are difficulties fufficient to ftagger credulity itfelf ; and at length produced the enquiries of Dr. Hunter. That celebrated anatomift, having procured fpecimens from the Ohio, examined them with that accuracy for which he is fo much diftinguifhed. He difcovered a confiderable difference between the fhape and ftructure of the bones, and thofe of the elephant. He obferved from the form of the teeth, that they muft have belonged to a carnivorous animal ; whereas the habits of the elephant are foreign to
fuch

such sustenance, and his jaws totally unprovided with the teeth necessary for its use : And from the whole he concluded to the satisfaction of naturalists, that these bones belonged to a quadruped now unknown, and whose race is probably extinct, unless it may be be found in the extensive continent of New Holland, whose recesses have not yet been pervaded by the curiosity or avidity of civilized man. Can then so great a link have perished from the chain of nature? Happy we that it has. How formidable an enemy to the human species, an animal as large as the elephant, the tyrant of the forests, perhaps the devourer of man! Nations, such as the Indians, must have been in perpetual alarm. The animosities among the various tribes must have been suspended till the common enemy, who threatened the very existence of all, should be extirpated. To this circumstance we are probably indebted for a fact, which is perhaps singular in its kind, the extinction of a whole race of animals from the system of nature.

RIGHTS of LAND.

THE proprietors of the Kentucke lands obtain their patents from Virginia, and their rights are of three kinds, viz. Those which arise from military service, from settlement and pre-emption, or from warrants from the treasury. The
military

military rights are held by officers, or their repre-
fentatives, as a reward for fervices done in one of
the two laft wars. The Settlement and pre-emption rights arife from occupation. Every man
who, before March, 1780, had remained in the
country one year, or raifed a crop of corn, was
allowed to have a fettlement of four hundred a-
cres, and a pre-emption adjoining it of one
thoufand acres. Every man who had only built
a cabbin, or made any improvement by himfelf or others, was entitled to a pre-emption
of one thoufand acres where fuch improvement
was made.

In March, 1780, the fettlement and pre-
emption rights ceafed, and treafury warrants were afterwards iffued, authorizing their
poffeffor to locate the quantity of land mentioned in them, wherever it could be found
vacant in Virginia.

The mode of procedure in thefe affairs may be
inftructive to the reader. After the entry is made
in the land-office, there being one in each county, the perfon making the entry takes out a copy of the location, and proceeds to furvey when
he pleafes. The plot and certificate of fuch furvey muft be returned to the office within three
months after the furvey is made, there to be re-
corded; and a copy of the record muft be taken
out

out in twelve months, after the return of the survey, and produced to the affiftant regifter of the land-office in Kentucke, where it muft lie fix months, that prior locators may have time and opportunity to enter a caveat, and prove their better right. If no caveat is entered in that time, the plot and certificate are fent to the land-office at Richmond, in Virginia, and three months more are allowed to have the patent returned to the owner.

The validity of the right of Virginia to this extenfive weftern territory has been difputed by fome, but without reafon. The weftern boundary of that ftate, by charter, reftricted by the treaty of Paris, in 1763, is fixed upon the Ohio River. She has purchafed the foil from the Indians, has firft fettled it, and eftablifhed wholefome laws for the regulation and government of the inhabitants; and therefore we conclude, that the right of Virginia to Kentucke is as permanent as the independence of America.

TRADE of KENTUCKE.

A CONVENIENT fituation for commerce is the grand hinge upon which the population, riches and happinefs of every country greatly depends. I believe many conceive the fituation of Kentucke to be unfavourable in this refpect. I confefs when I firft vifited this country I was

was of the opinion of other misinformed men, that the best channel was from Philadelphia or Baltimore, by the way of Pittsburg,* and from thence down the Ohio; and upon account of the difficulties and expences attending this route, for which there is no remedy, that goods would ever be dear. This opinion I have since reprobated, as the effect of ignorance of the trade up the Missississippi from New Orleans, or Mantchac, at the river or gut Iberville.

Those who are acquainted with America know the Mississippi and Ohio rivers to be the key to the northern parts of the western continent: These are the principal channels through which that extensive region, bathed by their waters, and enriched by the many streams they receive, communicate with the sea, and may truly be considered as the great passage made by the Hand of Nature for a variety of valuable purposes, and principally to promote the happiness and benefit of mankind; amongst which, the conveyance of the produce of that immense and fertile country lying westward of the United States is not the least. A short description of these rivers, and some others flowing into them, are objects submitted to the reader's attention, in order to form

a

---

* *From Philadelphia to Pittsburg is a land-carriage of* 320 *miles, from Baltimore* 280.

a juft idea of the favourable commercial circumftances of that important country.

The Ohio river begins at Pittfburg, 320 miles
weft of Philadelphia, being there formed by the
junction of the Alleghany and Monangehela rivers,
and running a winding courfe of S. 60° Weft,
falls into the Miffiffippi 1074 miles, by the meanders of the river, below Pittfburg. The only obftruc-
tion to navigation on this river are the Rapids,
as defcribed before under the defcription of the
Kentucke rivers; but they are paffed in fafety
when the ftream is high.

The moft remarkable branches compofing the
head waters of Ohio are Red-ftone Creek, Cheat
River, and Yochiaghany. Thefe waters are navigable to a confiderable diftance above Pittfburg,
from November until June, and the Ohio a
month longer; but from great Kenhawa, which
is one hundred and ninety-fix miles and a half below Pittfburg, the ftream is navigable moft of the
year. Down this river great quantities of goods
are brought, and fome are conveyed up the Kentucke rivers, others on horfe-back or in waggons
to the fettled parts, and fold on an average at one
hundred pounds per cent. advance.

The current of the Ohio defcends about two
miles an hour in autumn, and when the waters
are

are high, about five miles. Thofe of the Kentucke rivers are much the fame, and without rapids, and are of immenfe value to the country, affording fifh and fowl, and tranfportation of the produce of the country to the beft market. Thefe rivers increafe the Ohio more in depth than breadth. At its mouth it is not more than one and a half mile in width, and enters the Miffiffippi in a S. weft direction with a flow current, and a fine channel. This great river, at the junction with the Ohio, runs in a S. eaft direction, and afterwards in a S. weft, having been a little before joined by a greater river called Miffouri,* which runs in an eaftward direction through Louifiana, and afterwards communicates to the Miffiffippi‡ its own muddy and majeftic appearance. From the mouth of the Ohio to New Orleans, a diftance not exceeding 460 miles in a ftraight line, is about 856 by water. The depth is, in common, eight or ten fathoms until you approach its mouth, which empties itfelf by feveral channels into the gulf of Mexico. Here the navigation is dangerous, on account of the many iflands, fand-bars and logs, interfperfed in its mouth, which is about twenty miles wide.

F   This

---

* The Miffouri is fuppofed to be about 3000 miles long.

‡ The Miffiffippi is faid to be about 2500 miles long.

This difadvantage may be remedied almoft in the fame manner that the ftream was difconcerted. The conflict between the fea and this mighty river, which brings down with its ftream great numbers of trees, mud, leaves, &c. caufes them to fubfide and form fhoals. One of thefe trees, ftopped by its roots or branches, will foon be joined by thoufands more, and fo fixed, that no human force is able to remove them. In time they are confolidated, every flood adds another layer to their height, forming iflands, which at length are covered with fhrubs, grafs and cane, and forcibly fhift the bed of the river. In this manner we fuppofe moft of the country on each fide of the Miffiffippi, below the Iberville, to have been formed, by iflands uniting to iflands, which in a fucceffion of time have greatly encroached on the fea, and produced an extenfive tract of country. If fome of the floating timber at the mouths of this river were moved into fome of the channels, numbers more would incorporate with them; and the current being impeded in thefe, the whole force of the river uniting, one important channel would forceably be opened, and fufficiently cleared, to admit of the moft excellent navigation.

About ninety-nine miles above Orleans is a fort, now called Mantchac by the Spaniards; formerly Fort Bute by the Englifh, who built it. Near this is
a large

a large gut, formed by the Miffiffippi, on the eaft fide, called Iberville; fome have dignified it with the name of River, when the Miffiffippi, its fource, is high. This is navigable at moft not above four months in the year for the firft ten miles; for three miles further it is from two to fix feet in autumn, and from two to four fathoms the remaining part of the way to lake Maurepas, receiving in its courfe the river Amit, which is navigable for batteaux to a confiderable diftance.

Lake Maurepas is about ten miles in length, and feven in breadth; and there is a paffage of feven miles between this and Lake Pontchartrain.

Lake Pontchartrain is about forty miles long, twenty four broad, and eighteen feet deep. From this lake to the fea the channel is ten miles long, and three hundred yards wide; and the water deep enough to admit large veffels through thefe lakes, and their communications. This place, if attended to, might be of confequence to all the the weftern country, and to the commerce of Weft-Florida: For it may reafonably be fuppof-ed, that the inhabitants and traders of the weft-ern country would rather trade at this place than at New Orleans, if they could have as good re-turns for their peltry, and the produce of their foil, as it makes a confiderable difference in their voyage,

voyage, and faves labour, money and time. Experience will doubtlefs produce confiderable improvements, and render the navigation of the Miffiffippi, either by thefe lakes, or New Orleans, nearly as cheap as any other. That the Miffiffippi can anfwer every valuable purpofe of trade and commerce is proved already to a demonftration by experience.

I have reafon to believe that the time is not far diftant when New Orleans will be a great trading city, and perhaps another will be built near Mantchac, at Iberville, that may in time rival its glory.

A prodigious number of iflands, fome of which are of great extent, are interfperfed in that mighty river; and the difficulty in afcending it in the Spring when the floods are high, is compenfated by eddies or counter currents, which moftly run in the bends near the banks of the river with nearly equal velocity againft the ftream, and affift the afcending boats. This river is rapid in thofe parts which have clufters of iflands, fhoals and fand-banks; but the rapidity of thefe places will be no inconvenience to the newly invented mechanical boats,* it being their peculiar property to fail beft in fmart currents.

From

---

* *This plan is now in agitation in Virginia, and*

From New Orleans to the Falls of Ohio, batteaux, carrying about 40 tons, have been rowed
by eighteen or twenty men in eight or ten weeks,
which, at the extent, will not amount to more
than five hundred pounds expence, which experience has proved to be about one third of that
from Philadelphia. It is highly probable that in
time the diſtance will be exceedingly ſhortened by
cuting a-croſs bends of the river.

Charlevoix relates, that at Coupee or Cut-point,
the river formerly made a great turn, and ſome
Canadians, by deepening the channel of a ſmall
brook, diverted the waters of the river into it.
The impetuoſity of the ſtream was ſo violent, and
the ſoil of ſo rich and looſe a quality, that in a
ſhort time the point was entirely cut through,
and the old channel left dry, except in inunda-
tions, by which travellers ſave 14 leagues of their
voyage.

---

*recommended to government by two gentlemen of firſt
rate abilities, Mr. Charles Rumſey and Doct. James
McMacken. Their propoſals are, " to conſtruct a
ſpecies of boat, of the burthen of ten tons, that ſhall
ſail, or be propelled by the force of mechanical powers thereto applied, up the ſtream of a freſh water
river the diſtance of between 25 and 40 miles a
day, notwithſtanding the velocity of the water ſhould
move at the rate of 10 miles an hour, to be wrought
at no greater expence than that of three hands."*

voyage. The new channel has been founded with a line of thirty fathoms without finding bottom. When the diftance is fhortened, which I believe may readily be done, and the mechanical boats brought to their higheft improvement, the expences of a voyage from New Orleans to the Falls of Ohio will be attended with inconfiderable expence. Now we know by experience that forty tons of goods cannot be taken to the Falls of Ohio from Philadelphia under fixteen hundred pounds expence; but by improvements on the Miffiffippi, with the conveniences of thefe boats, goods can be brought from New Orleans to the Falls for the tenth part of that expence; and if they are fold at one hundred pounds per cent. now, when brought from Philadelphia at expences fo great, what may the merchant afford to fell his goods at, who brings them fo much cheaper? Befides, the great advantages arifing from the exporting of peltry, and country produce, which never can be conveyed to the eaftern ports to any advantage. It is evident alfo that the market from which they receive imports, muft confequently receive their exports, which is the only return they can poffibly make.

By ftating the commerce of Kentucke in its proper terms, we find the expences fuch, that we conclude with propriety, that that country will be be fupplied with goods as cheap as if fituated but forty miles from Philadelphia.

But perhaps it will be replied, New Orleans is in the poffeflion of the Spaniards, who, whenever they pleafe, may make ufe of that fort, and fome others they have on the Miffiffippi, to prevent the navigation, and ruin the trade. The paffage through Iberville is alfo fubject to the Spaniards, and befides, inconvenient ; that ftream continuing fo fhort a time, and in the moft difadvantageous feafon.

I grant it will be abfurd to expect a free navigation of the Miffiffippi whilft the Spaniards are in poffeffion of New Orleans. To fuppofe it, is an idea calculated to impofe only upon the weak. They may perhaps trade with us upon their own terms, while they think it confiftent with their intereft,* but no friendfhip in trade exifts when intereft expires ; therefore, when the weftern country becomes populous and ripe for trade, found policy tells us the Floridas muft be ours too. According to the articles of the Definitive Treaty, we are to have a free and unmolefted navigation
of

* *Article 8th of the late Definitive Treaty, fays, The navigation of the Miffiffippi River from its fource to the ocean, fhall for ever remain free and open to the fubjects of Great-Britain and the citizens of the United States.*

of the Miſſiſſippi; but experience teaches mankind that treaties are not always to be depended on, the moſt ſolemn being broken. Hence we learn that no one ſhould put much faith in any ſtate; and the trade and commerce of the Miſſiſſippi River cannot be ſo well ſecured in any other poſſeſſion as our own.

Although the Iberville only admits of a ſhort and inconvenient navigation, yet if a commercial town were built there, it would be the center of the weſtern trade; and a land carriage of ten or twelve miles would be counted no diſadvantage to the merchant. Nay, I doubt not, that in time a canal will be broke through the gut of Iberville, which may divert the water of Miſſiſſippi that way, and render it a place of the greateſt conſequence in America; but this important period is reſerved for futurity.

APPENDIX:

APPENDIX.

The ADVENTURES of Col. DA-NIEL BOON; containing a NARRA-TIVE of the WARS of Kentucke.

CURIOSITY is natural to the foul of man, and interefting objects have a powerful influence on our affections. Let thefe influencing powers actuate, by the permiffion or difpofal of Providence, from felfifh or focial views, yet in time the myfterious will of Heaven is unfolded, and we behold our conduct, from whatfoever motives excited, operating to anfwer the important defigns of heaven. Thus we behold Kentucke, lately an howling wildernefs, the habitation of favages and wild beafts, become a fruitful field; this region, fo favourably diftinguifhed by nature, now become the habitation of civilization,

G   at

at a period unparalleled in hiftory, in the midft of a raging war, and under all the difadvantages of emigration to a country fo remote from the inhabited parts of the continent. Here, where the hand of violence fhed the blood of the innocent ; where the horrid yells of favages, and the groans of the diftreffed, founded in our ears, we now hear the praifes and adorations of our Creator ; where wretched wigwams ftood, the miferable abodes of favages, we behold the foundations of cities laid, that, in all probability, will rival the glory of the greateft upon earth. And we view Kentucke fituated on the fertile banks of the great Ohio, rifing from obfcurity to fhine with fplendor, equal to any other of the ftars of the American hemifphere.

The fettling of this region well deferves a place in hiftory. Moft of the memorable events I have myfelf been exercifed in ; and, for the fatisfaction of the public, will briefly relate the circumftances of my adventures, and fcenes of life, from my firft movement to this country until this day.

It was on the firft of May, in the year 1769, that I refigned my domeftic happinefs for a time, and left my family and peaceable habitation on the Yadkin River, in North-Carolina, to wander through the wildernefs of America, in queft of
the

the country of Kentucke, in company with John Finley, John Stewart, Joseph Holden, James Monay, and William Cool. We proceeded fuccefsfully, and after a long and fatiguing journey through a mountainous wildernefs, in a weftward direction, on the feventh day of June following, we found ourfelves on Red-River, where John Finley had for merly been trading with the Indians, and, from the top of an eminence, faw with pleafure the beautiful level of Kentucke. Here let me obferve, that for fome time we had experienced the moft uncomfortable weather as a prelibation of our future fufferings. At this place we encamped, and made a fhelter to defend us from the inclement feafon, and began to hunt and reconnoitre the country. We found every where abundance of wild beafts of all forts, through this vaft foreft. The buffaloes were more frequent than I have feen cattle in the fettlements, browzing on the leaves of the cane, or croping the herbage on thofe extenfive plains, fearlefs, becaufe ignorant, of the violence of man. Sometimes we faw hundreds in a drove, and the numbers about the falt fprings were amazing. In this foreft, the habitation of beafts of every kind natural to America, we practifed hunting with great fuccefs until the twenty-fecond day of December following.

This day John Stewart and I had a pleafing
ramble,

ramble, but fortune changed the scene in the close of it. We had passed through a great forest, on which stood myriads of trees, some gay with blossoms, others rich with fruits. Nature was here a series of wonders, and a fund of delight. Here she displayed her ingenuity and industry in a variety of flowers and fruits, beautifully coloured, elegantly shaped, and charmingly flavoured; and we were diverted with innumerable animals presenting themselves perpetually to our view.—In the decline of the day, near Kentucke river, as we ascended the brow of a small hill, a number of Indians rushed out of a thick cane-brake upon us, and made us prisoners. The time of our sorrow was now arrived, and the scene fully opened. The Indians plundered us of what we had, and kept us in confinement seven days, treating us with common savage usage. During this time we discovered no uneasiness or desire to escape, which made them less suspicious of us; but in the dead of night, as we lay in a thick cane-brake by a large fire, when sleep had locked up their senses, my situation not disposing me for rest, I touched my companion and gently awoke him. We improved this favourable opportunity, and departed, leaving them to take their rest, and speedily directed our course towards our old camp, but found it plundered, and the company dispersed and gone home. About this time

my

my brother, Squire Boon, with another adventurer, who came to explore the country shortly after us, was wandering through the forest, determined to find me, if possible, and accidentally found our camp. Notwithstanding the unfortunate circumstances of our company, and our dangerous situation, as surrounded with hostile savages, our meeting so fortunately in the wilderness made us reciprocally sensible of the utmost satisfaction. So much does friendship triumph over misfortune, that sorrows and sufferings vanish at the meeting not only of real friends, but of the most distant acquaintances, and substitutes happiness in their room.

Soon after this, my companion in captivity, John Stewart, was killed by the savages, and the man that came with my brother returned home by himself. We were then in a dangerous, helpless situation, exposed daily to perils and death amongst savages and wild beasts, not a white man in the country but ourselves.

Thus situated, many hundred miles from our families in the howling wilderness, I believe few would have equally enjoyed the happiness we experienced. I often observed to my brother, You see now how little nature requires to be satisfied. Felicity, the companion of content, is rather found in our own breasts than in the enjoyment of external things: And I firmly believe it requires
quires

quires but a little philofophy to make a man happy in whatfoever ftate he is. This confifts in a full refignation to the will of Providence; and a refigned foul finds pleafure in a path ftrewed with briars and thorns.

We continued not in a ftate of indolence, but hunted every day, and prepared a little cottage to defend us from the Winter ftorms. We remained there undifturbed during the Winter; and on the firft day of May, 1770, my brother returned home to the fettlement by himfelf, for a new recruit of horfes and ammunition, leaving me by myfelf, without bread, falt or fugar, without company of my fellow creatures, or even a horfe or dog. I confefs I never before was under greater neceffity of exercifing philofophy and fortitude. A few days I paffed uncomfortably. The idea of a beloved wife and family, and their anxiety upon the account of my abfence and expofed fituation, made fenfible impreffions on my heart. A thoufand dreadful apprehenfions prefented themfelves to my view, and had undoubtedly difpofed me to melancholy, if further indulged.

One day I undertook a tour through the country, and the diverfity and beauties of nature I met with in this charming feafon, expelled every gloomy and vexatious thought. Juft at the clofe of

of day the gentle gales retired, and left the place
to the difpofal of a profound calm. Not a breeze
fhook the moft tremulous leaf. I had gained the
fummit of a commanding ridge, and, looking
round with aftonifhing delight, beheld the ample
plains, the beauteous tracts below. On the other
hand, I furveyed the famous river Ohio that rolled
in filent dignity, marking the weftern boundary
of Kentucke with inconceivable grandeur. At a
vaft diftance I beheld the mountains lift their venerable brows, and penetrate the clouds. All
things were ftill. I kindled a fire near a foun-
tain of fweet water, and feafted on the loin of a
buck, which a few hours before I had killed.
The fullen fhades of night foon overfpread the
whole hemifphere, and the earth feemed to gafp
after the hovering moifture. My roving excurfion this day had fatigued my body, and diverted
my imagination. I laid me down to fleep, and I
awoke not until the fun had chafed away the
night. I continued this tour, and in a few days
explored a confiderable part of the country,
each day equally pleafed as the firft. I returned
again to my old camp, which was not difturbed
in my abfence. I did not confine my lodging to
it, but often repofed in thick cane-brakes, to a-
void the favages, who, I believe, often vifited my
camp, but fortunately for me, in my abfence. In
this fituation I was conftantly expofed to danger,
and death. How unhappy fuch a fituation for
a man

a man tormented with fear, which is vain if no
danger comes, and if it does, only augments the
pain. It was my happineſs to be deſtitute of this
afflicting paſſion, with which I had the greateſt
reaſon to be affected. The prowling wolves diverted my nocturnal hours with perpetual howl-
ings; and the various ſpecies of animals in this vaſt
foreſt, in the day time, were continually in my view.

Thus I was ſurrounded with plenty in the midſt
of want. I was happy in the midſt of dangers
and inconveniences. In ſuch a diverſity it was
impoſſible I ſhould be diſpoſed to melancholy. No
populous city, with all the varieties of commerce
and ſtately ſtructures, could afford ſo much plea-
ſure to my mind, as the beauties of nature I found
here.

Thus, through an uninterrupted ſcene of ſyl-
van pleaſures, I ſpent the time until the 27th
day of July following, when my brother, to my
great felicity, met me, according to appointment,
at our old camp. Shortly after, we left this place,
not thinking it ſafe to ſtay there longer, and proceeded to Cumberland river, reconnoitring that
part of the country until March, 1771, and
giving names to the different waters.

Soon after, I returned home to my family with a determination to bring them as ſoon as
                                            poſſible

poffible to live in Kentucke, which I efteemed a
fecond paradife, at the rifk of my life and fortune.

I returned fafe to my old habitation, and found
my family in happy circumftances. I fold my
farm on the Yadkin, and what goods we could
not carry with us ; and on the twenty-fifth day
of September, 1773, bade a farewel to our friends,
and proceeded on our journey to Kentucke, in
company with five families more, and forty men
that joined us in Powel's Valley, which is one
hundred and fifty miles from the now fettled parts
of Kentucke. This promifing beginning was
foon overcaft with a cloud of adverfity ; for upon the tenth day of October, the rear of our
company was attacked by a number of Indians,
who killed fix, and wounded one man. Of thefe
my eldeft fon was one that fell in the action.
Though we defended ourfelves, and repulfed the
enemy, yet this unhappy affair fcattered our cattle, brought us into extreme difficulty, and fo
difcouraged the whole company, that we retreated forty miles, to the fettlement on Clench
river. We had paffed over two mountains, viz.
Powel's and Walden's, and were approaching
Cumberland mountain when this adverfe fortune
overtook us. Thefe mountains are in the wildernefs, as we pafs from the old fettlements in
Virginia to Kentucke, are ranged in a S. weft and

H   N. eaft

N. east direction, are of a great length and breadth,
and not far distant from each other. Over these,
nature hath formed passes, that are less difficult
than might be expected from a view of such huge
piles. The aspect of these cliffs is so wild and
horrid, that it is impossible to behold them
without terror. The spectator is apt to imagine
that nature had formerly suffered some violent
convulsion; and that these are the dismembered
remains of the dreadful shock; the ruins, not
of Persepolis or Palmyra, but of the world!

I remained with my family on Clench until
the sixth of June, 1774, when I and one Mi-
chael Stoner were solicited by Governor Dunmore, of Virginia, to go to the Falls of the Ohio,
to conduct into the settlement a number of surveyors that had been sent thither by him some
months before; this country having about this
time drawn the attention of many adventurers.
We immediately complied with the Governor's request, and conducted in the surveyors, compleat-
ing a tour of eight hundred miles, through many difficulties, in sixty-two days.

Soon after I returned home, I was ordered to
take the command of three garrisons during the
campaign, which Governor Dunmore carried on a-
gainst the Shawanese Indians: After the conclu-
sion of which, the Militia was discharged from
each

each garrifon, and I being relieved from my poft, was folicited by a number of North-Carolina gentlemen, that were about purchafing the lands lying on the S. fide of Kentucke River, from the Cherokee Indians, to attend their treaty at Wataga, in March, 1775, to negotiate with them, and, mention the boundaries of the purchafe. This I accepted, and at the requeft of the fame gentlemen, undertook to mark out a road in the beft paffage from the fettlement through the wildernefs to Kentucke, with fuch affiftance as I thought neceffary to employ for fuch an important undertaking.

I foon began this work, having collected a number of enterprifing men, well armed   We proceeded with all poffible expedition until we came within fifteen miles of where Boonfborough now ftands, and where we were fired upon by a party of Indians that killed two, and wounded two of our number; yet, although furprifed and taken at a difadvantage, we ftood our ground. This was on the twentieth of March, 17 5. Three days after, we were fired upon again, and had two men killed, and three wounded.. Afterwards we proceeded on to Kentucke river without oppofition ; and on the fift day of April began to erect the fort of Boonfborough at a falt lick, about fixty yards from the river, on the S. fide.

On

On the fourth day, the Indians killed one of our men.—We were bufily employed in building this fort, until the fourteenth day of June following, without any farther oppofition from the Indians ; and having finifhed the works, I returned to my family, on Clench.

In a fhort time, I proceeded to remove my family from Clench to this garrifon ; where we arrived fafe without any other difficulties than fueh as are common to this paffage, my wife and daughter being the firft white women that ever ftood on the banks of Kentucke river.

On the twenty-fourth day of December following we had one man killed, and one wounded, by the Indians, who feemed determined to perfecute us for erecting this fortification.

On the fourteenth day of July, 1776, two of Col. Calaway's daughters, and one of mine, were taken prifoners near the fort. I immediately purfued the Indians, with only eight men, and on the fixteenth overtook them, killed two of the party, and recovered the girls. The fame day on which this attempt was made, the Indians divided themfelves into different parties, and attacked feveral forts, which were fhortly before this time erected, doing a great deal of mifchief. This was extremely diftreffing to the new fettlers. The
innocent

innocent hufbandman was fhot down, while bu-
fy cultivating the foil for his family's fupply.
Moft of the cattle around the ftations were deftroyed. They continued their hoftilities in this
manner until the fifteenth of April, 1777, when
they attacked Boonfborough with a party of a-
bove one hundred in number, killed one man,
and wounded four —Their lofs in this attack was
not certainly known to us.

On the fourth day of July following, a party
of about two hundred Indians attacked Boonfborough, killed one man, and wounded two.
They befieged us forty-eight hours; during
which time feven of them were killed, and at
laft, finding themfelves not likely to prevail, they
raifed the fiege, and departed.

The Indians had difpofed their warriors in different parties at this time, and attacked the different garrifons to prevent their affifting each
other, and did much injury to the diftreffed inhabitants.

On the nineteenth day of this month, Col.
Logan's fort was befieged by a party of about
two hundred Indians. During this dreadful fiege
they did a great deal of mifchief, diftreffed the
garrifon, in which were only fifteen men, killed
two, and wounded one. The enemies lofs was
uncertain,

uncertain, from the common practice which the Indians have of carrying off their dead in time of battle. Col. Harrod's fort was then defended by only fixty-five men, and Boonfborough by twenty-two, there being no more forts or white men in the country, except at the Falls, a confiderable diftance from thefe, and all taken collectively, were but a handful to the numerous warriors that were every where difperfed through the country, intent upon doing all the mifchief that favage barbarity could invent. Thus we paffed through a fcene of fufferings that exceeds defcription.

On the twenty-fifth of this month a reinforcement of forty-five men arrived from North-Carolina, and about the twentieth of Auguft following, Col. Bowman arrived with one hundred men from Virginia. Now we began to ftrengthen, and from hence, for the fpace of fix weeks, we had fkirmifhes with Indians, in one quarter or other, almoft every day.

The favages now learned the fuperiority of the Long Knife, as they call the Virginians, by experience; being out-generalled in almoft every battle. Our affairs began to wear a new afpect, and the enemy, not daring to venture on open war, practifed fecret michief at times.

On

On the firſt day of January, 1778, I went with a party of thirty men to the Blue Licks, on Licking River, to make ſalt for the different garriſons in the country.

On the ſeventh day of February, as I was hunting, to procure meat for the company, I met with a party of one hundred and two Indians, and two Frenchmen, on their march againſt Boonſborough, that place being particularly the object of the enemy.

They purſued, and took me; and brought me on the eighth day to the Licks, where twenty-ſeven of my party were, three of them having previouſly returned home with the ſalt. I knowing it was impoſſible for them to eſcape, capitulated with the enemy, and, at a diſtance in their view, gave notice to my men of their ſituation, with orders not to reſiſt, but ſurrender themſelves captives.

The generous uſage the Indians had promiſed before in my capitulation, was afterwards fully complied with, and we proceeded with them as priſoners to old Chelicothe, the principal Indian town, on Little Miami, where we arrived, after an uncomfortable journey, in very ſevere weather, on the eighteenth day of February, and received as good treatment as priſoners could expect from ſavages.

vages.—On the tenth day of March following, I, and ten of my men, were conducted by forty Indians to Detroit, where we arrived the thirtieth day, and were treated by Governor Hamilton, the Britifh commander at that poft, with great humanity.

During our travels, the Indians entertained me well; and their affection for me was fo great, that they utterly refufed to leave me there with the others, although the Governor offered them one hundred pounds Sterling for me, on purpofe to give me a parole to go home. Several Englifh gentlemen there, being fenfible of my adverfe fortune, and touched with human fympathy, generoufly offered a friendly fupply for my wants, which I refufed, with many thanks for their kindnefs; adding, that I never expected it would be in my power to recompenfe fuch unmerited generofity.

The Indians left my men in captivity with the Britifh at Detroit, and on the tenth day of April brought me towards Old Chelicothe, where we arrived on the twenty-fifth day of the fame month. This was a long and fatiguing march, through an exceeding fertile country, remarkable for fine fprings and ftreams of water. At Chelicothe I fpent my time as comfortably as I could expect; was adopted, accordin to their cuftom,

into

into a family where I became a son, and had a great fhare in the affection of my new parents, brothers, fifters, and friends. I was exceedingly familiar and friendly with them, always appearing as chearful and fatisfied as poffible, and they put great confidence in me. I often went a hunting with them, and frequently gained their applaufe for my activity at our fhooting-matches. I was careful not to exceed many of them in fhooting; for no people are more envious than they in this fport. I could obferve, in their countenances and geftures, the greateft expreffions of joy when they exceeded me; and, when the reverfe happened, of envy. The Shawanefe king took great notice of me, and treated me with profound refpect, and entire friendfhip, often entrufting me to hunt at my liberty. I frequently returned with the fpoils of the woods, and as often prefented fome of what I had taken to him, expreffive of duty to my fovereign. My food and lodging was, in common, with them, not fo good indeed as I could defire, but neceffity made every thing acceptable.

I now began to meditate an efcape, and carefully avoided their fufpicions, continuing with them at Old Chelicothe until the firft day of June following, and then was taken by them to the falt fprings on Sciotha, and kept there, making falt, ten days. During this time I hunted

I   fome

some for them, and found the land, for a great extent about this river, to exceed the soil of Kentucke, if possible, and remarkably well watered.

When I returned to Chelicothe, alarmed to see four hundred and fifty Indians, of their choicest warriors, painted and armed in a fearful manner, ready to march against Boonsborough, I determined to escape the first opportunity.

On the sixteenth, before sun-rise, I departed in the most secret manner, and arrived at Boonsborough on the twentieth, after a journey of one hundred and sixty miles; during which, I had but one meal.

I found our fortress in a bad state of defence, but we proceeded immediately to repair our flanks, strengthen our gates and posterns, and form double bastions, which we compleated in ten days. In this time we daily expected the arrival of the Indian army ; and at length, one of my fellow prisoners, escaping from them, arrived, informing us that the enemy had an account of my departure, and postponed their expedition three weeks.—The Indians had spies out viewing our movements, and were greatly alarmed with our increase in number and fortifications. The Grand Councils of the nations were held frequently, and with more deliberation than usual. They evidently

dently faw the approaching hour when the Long Knife would difpoffefs them of their defirable habitations; and anxioufly concerned for futurity, determined utterly to extirpate the whites out of Kentucke. We were not intimidated by their movements, but frequently gave them proofs of our courage.

About the firft of Auguft, I made an incurfion into the Indian country, with a party of nineteen men, in order to furprife a fmall town, up Sciotha, called Paint-Creek-Town. We advanced within four miles thereof, where we met a party of thirty Indians, on their march againft Boonfborough, intending to join the others from Chelicothe. A fmart fight enfued betwixt us for fome time : At length the favages gave way, and fled. We had no lofs on our fide :, The enemy had one killed, and two wounded. We took from them three horfes, and all their baggage ; and being informed, by two of our number that went to their town, that the Indians had entirely evacuated it, we proceeded no further, and returned with all poffible expedition to affift our garrifon againft the other party. We paffed by them on the fixth day, and on the feventh, we arrived fafe at Boonfborough.

On the eighth, the Indian army arrived, being four hundred and forty-four in number, commanded
by

by Capt. Duquefne, eleven other Frenchmen, and fome of their own chiefs, and marched up within view of our fort, with Britifh and French colours flying; and having fent a fummons to me, in his Britannick Majefty's name, to furrender the fort, I requefted two days confideration, which was granted.

It was now a critical period with us.—We were a fmall number in the garrifon.—A powerful army before our walls, whofe appearance proclaimed inevitable death, fearfully painted, and marking their footfteps with defolation. Death was preferable to captivity; and if taken by ftorm, we muft inevitably be devoted to deftruction. In this fituation we concluded to maintain our garrifon, if poffible. We immediately proceeded to collect what we could of our horfes, and other cattle, and bring them through the pofterns into the fort: And in the evening of the ninth, I returned anfwer, that we were determined to defend our fort while a man was living.—Now, faid I to their commander, who ftood attentively hearing my fentiments, We laugh at all your formidable preparations: But thank you for giving us notice and time to provide for our defence. Your efforts will not prevail; for our gates fhall for ever deny you admittance.—Whether this anfwer affected their courage, or not, I cannot tell; but, contrary to our expectations, they
formed

formed a fcheme to deceive us, declaring it was
their orders, from Governor Hamilton, to take
us captives, and not to deftroy us; but if nine of
us would come out, and treat with them, they
would immediatly withdraw their forces from our
walls, and return home peaceably. This founded grateful in our ears; and we agreed to the
propofal.

We held the treaty within fixty yards of the
garrifon, on purpofe to divert them from a breach
of honour, as we could not avoid fufpicions of
the favages. In this fituation the articles were
formally agreed to, and figned; and the Indians
told us it was cuftomary with them, on fuch occa-
fions, for two Indians to fhake hands with every
white-man in the treaty, as an evidence of entire friendfhip. We agreed to this alfo, but were
foon convinced their policy was to take us prifoners.—They immediately grappled us; but,
although furrounded by hundreds of favages, we
extricated ourfelves from them, and efcaped all
fafe into the garrifon, except one that was
wounded, through a heavy fire from their army.
They immediately attacked us on every fide, and
a conftant heavy fire enfued between us day and
night for the fpace of nine days.

In this time the enemy began to undermine our
fort, which was fituated fixty yards from Kentucke

tucke river. They began at the water-mark, and proceeded in the bank some diftance, which we underftood by their making the water muddy with the clay; and we immediately proceeded to difappoint their defign, by cutting a trench a-crofs their fubterranean paffage. The enemy difcovering our counter-mine, by the clay we threw out of the fort, defifted from that ftratagem : And experience now fully convincing them that neither their power nor policy could effect their purpofe, on the twentieth day of Auguft they raifed the fiege, and departed.

During this dreadful fiege, which threatened death in every form, we had two men killed, and four wounded, befides a number of cattle. We killed of the enemy thirty-feven, and wounded a great number. After they were gone, we picked up one hundred and twenty-five pounds weight of bullets, befides what ftuck in the logs of our fort; which certainly is a great proof of their induftry. Soon after this, I went into the fettlement, and nothing worthy of a place in this account paffed in my affairs for fome time.

During my abfence from Kentucke, Col. Bowman carried on an expedition againft the Shawanefe, at Old Chelicothe, with one hundred and fixty men, in July, 1779. Here they arrived undifcovered, and a battle enfued, which lafted until

til ten o'clock, A. M. when Col. Bowman, finding he could not fucceed at this time, retreated about thirty miles. The Indians, in the mean time, collecting all their forces, purfued and overtook him, when a fmart fight continued near two hours, not to the advantage of Col. Bowman's party.

Col. Harrod propofed to mount a number of horfe, and furioufly to rufh upon the favages, who at this time fought with remarkable fury. This defperate ftep had a happy effect, broke their line of battle, and the favages fled on all fides. In thefe two battles we had nine killed, and one wounded. The enemy's lofs uncertain, only two fcalps being taken.

On the twenty-fecond day of June, 1780, a large party of Indians and Canadians, about fix hundred in number, commanded by Col. Bird, attacked Riddle's and Martin's ftations, at the Forks of Licking River, with fix pieces of artillery. They carried this expedition fo fecretly, that the unwary inhabitants did not difcover them, until they fired upon the forts; and, not being prepared to oppofe them, were obliged to furrender themfelves miferable captives to barbarous favages, who immediately after tomahawked one man and two women, and loaded all the others with heavy baggage, forcing them along toward

toward their towns, able or unable to march.
Such as were weak and faint by the way, they
tomahawked. The tender women, and helpless
children, fell victims to their cruelty. This, and
the savage treatment they received afterwards, is
shocking to humanity, and too barbarous to relate.

The hostile disposition of the savages, and their
allies, caused General Clark, the commandant at
the Falls of the Ohio, immediately to begin an
expedition with his own regiment, and the armed force of the country, against Pecaway, the
principal town of the Shawanese, on a branch of
Great Miami, which he finished with great suc-
cess, took seventeen scalps, and burnt the town
to ashes, with the loss of seventeen men.

About this time I returned to Kentucke with
my family; and here, to avoid an enquiry into
my conduct, the reader being before informed of
my bringing my family to Kentucke, I am under
the necessity of informing him that, during my
captivity with the Indians, my wife, who de-
spaired of ever seeing me again, expecting the Indians had put a period to my life, oppressed with
the distresses of the country, and bereaved of me,
her only happiness, had, before I returned, trans-
ported my family and goods, on horses, through
the wilderness, amidst a multitude of dangers,
to her father's house, in North-Carolina.

Shortly

Shortly after the troubles at Boonfborough, I went to them, and lived peaceably there until this time. The hiftory of my going home, and returning with my family, forms a feries of difficulties, an account of which would fwell a volume, and being foreign to my purpofe, I fhall purpofely omit them.

I fettled my family in Boonfborough once more; and fhortly after, on the fixth day of October, 1780, I went in company with my brother to the Blue Licks ; and, on our return home, we were fired upon by a party of Indians. They fhot him, and purfued me, by the fcent of their dog, three miles ; but I killed the dog, and efcaped. The Winter foon came on, and was very fevere, which confined the Indians to their wigwams.

The feverity of this Winter caufed great difficulties in Kentucke. The enemy had deftroyed moft of the corn, the Summer before. This neceffary article was fcarce, and dear ; and the inhabitants lived chiefly on the flefh of buffaloes. The circumftances of many were very lamentable : However, being a hardy race of people, and accuftomed to difficulties and neceffities, they were wonderfully fupported through all their fufferings, until the enfuing Fall, when we received abundance from the fertile foil.

K   Towards

Towards Spring, we were frequently haraffed by Indians; and, in May, 1782, a party affaulted Afhton's ftation, killed one man, and took a Negro prifoner. Capt. Afhton, with twenty-five men, purfued, and overtook the favages, and a fmart fight enfued, which lafted two hours; but they being fuperior in number, obliged Captain Afhton's party to retreat, with the lofs of eight killed, and four mortally wounded; their brave commander himfelf being numbered among the dead.

The Indians continued their hoftilities; and, about the tenth of Auguft following, two boys were taken from Major Hoy's ftation. This party was purfued by Capt. Holder and feventeen men, who were alfo defeated, with the lofs of four men killed, and one wounded. Our affairs became more and more alarming. Several ftations which had lately been erected in the country were continually infefted with favages, ftealing their horfes and killing the men at every opportunity. In a field, near Lexington, an Indian fhot a man, and running to fcalp him, was himfelf fhot from the fort, and fell dead upon his enemy.

Every day we experienced recent mifchiefs. The barbarous favage nations of Shawanefe, Cherokees, Wyandots, Tawas, Delawares, and feveral others near Detroit, united in a war againft us,

us, and affembled their choiceft warriors at old
Chelicothe, to go on the expedition, in order to
deftroy us, and entirely depopulate the country.
Their favage minds were inflamed to mifchief
by two abandoned men, Captains M'Kee and
Girty. Thefe led them to execute every diaboli-
cal fcheme ; and, on the fifteenth day of Auguft,
commanded a party of Indians and Canadians,
of about five hundred in number, againft Bri-
ant's ftation, five miles from Lexington. Without demanding a furrender, they furioufly affaulted the garrifon, which was happily prepared
to oppofe them ; and, after they had expended
much ammunition in vain, and killed the cattle
round the fort, not being likely to make themfelves mafters of this place, they raifed the fiege,
and departed in the morning of the third day after they came, with the lofs of about thirty killed, and the number of wounded uncertain.—Of
the garrifon four were killed, and three wounded.

On the eighteenth day Col. Todd, Col. Trigg,
Major Harland, and myfelf, fpeedily collected
one hundred and feventy-fix men, well armed,
and purfued the favages. They had marched beyond the Blue Licks to a remarkable bend of the
main fork of Licking River, about forty-three
miles from Lexington, as it is particularly reprefented in the map, where we overtook them on
the

the nineteenth day. The favages obferving us, gave way ; and we, being ignorant of their numbers, paffed the river. When the enemy faw our proceedings, having greatly the advantage of us in fituation, they formed the line of battle, as reprefented in the map, from one bend of Licking to the other, about a mile from the Blue Licks. An exceeding fierce battle immediately began, for about fifteen minutes, when we, being over-powered by numbers, were obliged to retreat, with the lofs of fixty-feven men ; feven of whom were taken prifoners. The brave and much lamented Colonels Todd and Trigg, Major Harland and my fecond fon, were among the dead. We were informed, that the Indians, numbering their dead, found they had four killed more than we ; and therefore, four of the prifoners they had taken, were, by general confent, ordered to be killed, in a moft barbarous manner, by the young warriors, in order to train them up to cruelty ; and then they proceeded to their towns.

On our retreat we were met by Col. Logan, haftening to join us, with a number of well armed men: This powerful affiftance we unfortunately wanted in the battle; for, notwithftanding the enemy's fuperiority of numbers, they acknowledged that, if they had received one more fire from us, they fhould undoubtedly have given way. So valiantly did our fmall party fight, that,

that, to the memory of thofe who unfortunately fell in the battle, enough of honour cannot
be paid. Had Col. Logan and his party been
with us, it is highly probable we fhould have
given the favages a total defeat.

I cannot reflect upon this dreadful fcene, but
forrow fills my heart. A zeal for the defence of
their country led thefe heroes to the fcene of action, though with a few men to attack a powerful army of experienced warriors. When we
gave way, they purfued us with the utmoft ea-
gernefs, and in every quarter fpread deftruction.
The river was difficult to crofs, and many were
killed in the flight, fome juft entering the river,
fome in the water, others after croffing in afcending the cliffs. Some efcaped on horfe-back, a
few on foot ; and, being difperfed every where,
in a few hours, brought the melancholy news of
this unfortunate battle to Lexington. Many wi-
dows were now made. The reader may guefs
what forrow filled the hearts of the inhabitants,
exceeding any thing that I am able to defcribe.
Being reinforced, we returned to bury the dead,
and found their bodies ftrewed every where, cut
and mangled in a dreadful manner. This mourn-
ful fcene exhibited a horror almoft unparalleled :
Some torn and eaten by wild beafts ; thofe in the
river eaten by fifhes ; all in fuch a putrified con-
dition,

dition, that no one could be diftinguifhed from another.

As foon as General Claik, then at the Falls of the Ohio, who was ever our ready friend, and merits the love and gratitude of all his country-men, underftood the circumftances of this unfortunate action, he ordered an expedition, with all poffible hafte, to purfue the favages, which was fo expeditioufly effected, that we overtook them within two miles of their towns, and probably might have obtained a great victory, had not two of their number met us about two hundred poles before we come up. Thefe returned quick as lightening to their camp with the alarming news of a mighty army in view. The favages fled in the utmoft diforder, evacuated their towns, and reluctantly left their territory to our mercy. We immediately took poffeffion of Old Chelicothe without oppofition, being deferted by its inhabitants. We continued our purfuit through five towns on the Miami rivers, Old Chelicothe, Pecaway, New Chelicothe, Will's Towns, and Chelicothe, burnt them all to afhes, entirely deftroyed their corn, and other fruits, and every where fpread a fcene of defolation in the country. In this expedition we took feven prifoners and five fcalps, with the lofs of only four men, two of whom were accidentally killed by our own army.

This

This campaign in fome meafure damped the fpirits of the Indians, and made them fenfible of our fuperiority. Their connections were diffolved, their armies fcattered, and a future invafion put entirely out of their power ; yet they continued to practife mifchief fecretly upon the inhabitants, in the expofed parts of the country.

In October following, a party made an excurfion into that diftrict called the Crab Orchard, and one of them, being advanced fome diftance before the others, boldly entered the houfe of a poor defencelefs family, in which was only a Negro man, a woman and her children, terrified with the apprehenfions of immediate death. The favage, perceiving their defencelefs fituation, without offering violence to the family attempted to captivate the Negro, who, happily proved an over-match for him, threw him on the ground, and, in the ftruggle, the mother of the children drew an ax from a corner of the cottage, and cut his head off, while her little daughter fhut the door. The favages inftantly appeared, and applied their tomahawks to the door. An old rufty gun-barrel, without a lock, lay in a corner, which the mother put through a fmall crevice, and the favages, perceiving it, fled. In the mean time, the alarm fpread through the neighbourhood ; the armed men collected immediately, and purfued the ravagers into the wildernefs. Thus Providence,

Providence, by the means of this Negro, faved the whole of the poor family from deftruction. From that time, until the happy return of peace between the United States and Great-Britain, the Indians did us no mifchief. Finding the great king beyond the water difappointed in his expectations, and confcious of the importance of the Long Knife, and their own wretchednefs, fome of the nations immediately defired peace; to which, at prefent, they feem univerfally difpofed, and are fending ambaffadors to General Clark, at the Falls of the Ohio, with the minutes of their Councils; a fpecimen of which, in the minutes of the Piankafhaw Council, is fubjoined.

To conclude, I can now fay that I have verified the faying of an old Indian who figned Col. Henderfon's deed. Taking me by the hand, at the delivery thereof, Brother, fays he, we have given you a fine land, but I believe you will have much trouble in fettling it.—My footfteps have often been marked with blood, and therefore I can truly fubfcribe to its original name. Two darling fons, and a brother, have I loft by favage hands, which have alfo taken from me forty valuable horfes, and abundance of cattle. Many dark and fleeplefs nights have I been a companion for owls, feparated from the chearful fociety of men, fcorched by the Summer's fun, and pinched

pinched by the Winter's cold, an inftrument or-
dained to fettle the wildernefs. But now the
fcene is changed : Peace crowns the fylvan fhade.

What thanks, what ardent and ceafelefs thanks
are due to that all-fuperintending Providence
which has turned a cruel war into peace, brought
order out of confufion, made the fierce favages
placid, and turned away their hoftile weapons
from our country ! May the fame Almighty
Goodnefs banifh the accurfed monfter, war,
from all lands, with her hated affociates, rapine
and infatiable ambition. Let peace, defcending
from her native heaven, bid her olives fpring a-
midft the joyful nations; and plenty, in league
with commerce, fcatter bleffings from her copi-
ous hand.

This account of my adventures will inform
the reader of the moft remarkable events of this
country.—I now live in peace and fafety, enjoying the fweets of liberty, and the bounties of
Providence, with my once fellow-fufferers, in
this delightful country, which I have feen purchafed with a vaft expence of blood and treafure,
delighting in the profpect of its being, in a fhort
time, one of the moft opulent and powerful
ftates on the continent of North-America; which,
with the love and gratitude of my country-men,

L   I efteem

I esteem a sufficient reward for all my toil and dangers.

DANIEL BOON.

Fayette county, Kentucke.

PIANKASHAW COUNCIL.

In a COUNCIL, *held with the Piankashaw Indians, by Thomas J. Dalton, at Post St. Vincent's, April* 15, 1784.

MY CHILDREN,

WHAT I have often told you, is now come to pass. This day I received news from my Great Chief, at the Falls of Ohio. Peace is made with the enemies of America. The White Flesh, the Americans, French, Spaniards, Dutch and English, this day smoke out

of

of the peace-pipe. The tomahawk is buried, and they are now friends.

I am told the Shawanefe, Delawares, Chica-faws, Cherokees, and all other the Red Flefh, have taken the Long Knife by the hand. They have given up to them the prifoners that were in their nations.

My Children on Wabafh,
Open your ears, and let what I tell you fink deep in your hearts. You know me. Near twenty years I have been among you. The Long Knife is my nation. I know their hearts; peace they carry in one hand, and war in the other.

I leave you to yourfelves to judge. Confider, and now accept the one, or the other. We never beg peace of our enemies. If you love your women and children, receive the belt of wampum I prefent you. Return me my flefh you have in your villages, and the horfes you ftole from my people at Kentucke. Your corn-fields were never difturbed by the Long Knife. Your women and children lived quiet in their houfes, while your warriors were killing and robbing my people. All this you know is the truth. This is the laft time I fhall fpeak to you. I have waited fix moons to hear you fpeak, and to get my people from you. In ten nights I fhall
leave

leave the Wabaſh to ſee my Great Chief at the
Falls of Ohio, where he will be glad to hear,
from your own lips, what you have to ſay. Here
is tobacco I give you : Smoke; and conſider what
I have ſaid.—Then I delivered one belt of blue
and white wampum; and ſaid, Piankaſhaw,
ſpeak, ſpeak to the Americans.

Then the Piankaſhaw Chief anſwered;

My Great Father, the Long Knife,
You have been many years among us. You
have ſuffered by us. We ſtill hope you will have
pity and compaſſion upon us, on our women
and children; the day is clear. The ſun ſhines
on us; and the good news of peace appears in
our faces. This day, my Father, this is the day
of joy to the Wabaſh Indians. With one tongue
we now ſpeak.

We accept your peace-belt. We return God
thanks, you are the man that delivered us what
we long wiſhed for, peace, with the White
Fleſh. My Father, we have many times counſel-
led before you knew us; and you know how
ſome of us ſuffered before.

We received the tomahawk from the Engliſh :
Poverty forced us to it : We were attended by
other nations : We are ſorry for it. We this
day collect the bones of our friends that long a-
go were ſcattered upon the earth. We bury
them

them in one grave. We thus plant the tree of peace, that God may spread branches; so that we can all be secured from bad weather. They smoke as brothers out of the peace-pipe we now present you. Here, my Father, is the pipe that gives us joy. Smoke out of it. Our warriors are glad you are the man we present it to. You see, Father, we have buried the tomahawk: We now make a great chain of friendship never to be broken; and now, as one people, smoke out of your pipe. My Father, we know God was angry with us for stealing your horses, and disturbing your people. He has sent us so much snow and cold weather, that God himself killed all your horses, with our own.

We are now a poor people. God, we hope, will help us; and our Father, the Long Knife, will have pity and compassion on our women and children. Your flesh, my Father, is well that is among us; we shall collect them all together when they come in from hunting. Don't be sorry, my Father, all the prisoners taken at Kentucke are alive and well; we love them, and so do our young women.

Some of your people mend our guns, and others tell us they can make rum of the corn. Those are now the same as we. In one moon after this, we will go with them to their friends at Kentucke. Some of your people will now go
with

with Coftea, a Chief of our nation, to fee his Great Father, the Long Knife, at the Falls of Ohio.

My Father,

This being the day of joy to the Wabafh Indians, we beg a little drop of your milk, to let our warriors fee it came from your own breaft. We were born and raifed in the woods; we could never learn to make rum—God has made the White Flefh mafters of the world; they make every thing; and we all love rum————

Then they delivered three ftrings of blue and white wampum, and the coronet of peace.

PRESENT, in COUNCIL,

MUSKITO,
Capt. BEAVER,
WOODS & BURNING,
BADTRIPES,
ANTIA,
MONTOUR,
CASTIA,
GRAND COURT;

With many other Chiefs, and War Captains, and the Principal Inhabitants of the Poft of St. Vincent's.

O F

OF THE INDIANS.

WE have an account of twenty-eight different nations of Indians, Eaſtward of
the Miſſiſſippi.—Their ſituation is as follows.

The Cherokee Indians are neareſt to Kentucke, living upon the Teneſe River, near
the mouths of Clench, Holſtein, Nolachucke,
and French-Broad Rivers, which form the Teneſe or Cherokee River, in the interior parts of
North-Carolina, two hundred miles from Kentucke.

The Chicamawgees live about ninety miles
down the Teneſe from the Cherokees, at a place
called Chicamawgee, which in our language ſigni-
fies a Boiling Pot, there being a whirl-pool in
the river dangerous for boats. The Dragomo-
nough, a Chief of the Cherokees, with ſixty
more, broke off from that nation, and formed this
tribe,

tribe, which is called by the name of the Whirl-pool.

The Cheegees, and Middle-Settlement Indians, are settled about fifty and eighty miles South of the Cherokees.—These four tribes speak one language, being descended from the Cherokees.

The Chicasaws inhabit about one hundred miles N. W. from our settlement at French Lick, on Cumberland River, on the heads of a river called Tombeche, which runs into Mobile Bay.

The Choctaw nation are eighty miles from the Chicasaws, down the same river.

The Creek Indians live about one hundred and sixty miles South of the Choctaws, on the Apalache River, which runs into the Gulph of Mexico, some little distance East of Mobile Bay.

The Uchees Indians occupy four different places of residence, at the head of St. John's, the Fork of St. Mary's, the head of Cannuchee, and the head of St. Tillis. These rivers rise on the borders of Georgia, and run separately into the ocean.

The Catauba Indians are settled in North-Ca-rolina,

rolina, about two hundred miles diftant from Charles-town, in S. Carolina.

The tribes to the Weftward of Ohio River are the Delawares, living upon the Mifkingum River, which runs into the Ohio one hundred and eighty-feven miles above Sciotha, on the N. Weft fide.

The Mingo Nation lives upon a N. W. branch of Sciotha River, as is reprefented in the map.

The Wyandotts poffefs the banks of a river called Sandufky, which heads and interlocks with Sciotha, and, running in a contrary direction nearly N. W. for a great diftance, falls into Lake Erie.

The Six Nations are fettled upon waters running into Lake Ontario, that head in the mountain, from whence the Ohio and Sufquehannah rivers rife.

The Shawanefe Indians occupy five towns on the waters of Little and Great Miami, as appears in the map.

The Gibbaways are fixed on the Eaft fide of Detroit River, and oppofite the fort of that name. This river runs out of Lake Huron

M   into

into Lake Erie, is thirty-six miles in length, and the fort stands on the West side, half way betwixt these lakes.

The Hurons live six miles from the Gibbaways, towards Lake Huron, and on the same side of the river.

The Tawaws are found eighteen miles up the Mawmee or Omee River, which runs into Lake Erie.

There is a small tribe of Tawas settled at a place called the Rapids, some distance higher up the river than the former.

The Mawmee Indians live two hundred and forty miles up this river, at a place called Rosedebeau.

The Piankashaws reside about one hundred and sixty miles up Wabash River :—

The Vermilion Indians about sixty miles higher ;—and the Wyahtinaws about thirty miles still further up the same river.

The Wabash heads and interlocks with Mawmee, and runs a contrary direction into Ohio, three hundred and eighteen miles below the Falls.

The

The Long-isle or Isle-River Indians live on Isle, or White River, which runs into Wabash.

The Kickapoos are fixed on a branch of Mawmee River above the Long-isle Indians.

The Ozaw Nation lives on the Ozaw River, which runs into Mississippi :——

And the Kakasky Nation, on the Mississippi, two hundred miles above the Ozaws.

The Illinois Indians inhabit upon the Illinois River, which falls into the Mississippi ;——

And the Poutawottamies near St. Joseph's, a town on a branch of the Illinois.

The Sioux and Renards, are neighbours to the fort of Michillimackinac, on Lake Michigan.

These are the principal part of the Nations within the limits of the United States. Allowing about seven hundred to a nation or tribe, they will contain, in all, twenty thousand souls, and consequently may furnish between four and five thousand warriors.

The Speculations of curious idleness have framed
ed

ed many fyftems to account for the population
of this immenfe continent. There is fcarce a
people in the old world which has not had its
advocates; and there have not been wanting
fome, who, defpairing to loofen, have cut the
knot, by fuppofing that the power, which furnifhed America with plants, has in the fame
manner fupplied it with men, or at leaft, that
a remnant in this continent was faved from the
univerfal deluge, as well as in the other. As
this fubject is rather curious than ufeful, and, in its
very nature, does not admit of certainty, every thing
that paffed in America before the arrival of the
Europeans being plunged in Cimmerian darknefs,
except thofe little traditional records, which diffufe
a glimmering light on the two empires of Mexico and Peru, for about two hundred years at
moft before that period, we fhall only flightly
touch on that fubject; chiefly for the fake of
taking notice of fome modern difcoveries which
feem to ftrengthen the probability of fome former theories. The great fimilarity, or rather i-
dentity, of the perfons and manners of the A-
mericans, and thofe of the Tartars of the N.
Eaftern parts of Afia, together with a prefump-
tion, which has long poffeffed the learned,
that Afia and America were united, or at leaft feparated only by a narrow fea, has inclined the
more reflecting part of mankind to the opinion,
that the true origin of the Indians is from this
quarter. The immenfe feas, which feparate the
two

two continents on every other fide, render it high-ly improbable that any colonies could ever have been fent a-crofs them before the difcovery of the magnetical compafs. The ingenious M. Buffon too has remarked, and the obfervation appears to be juft, that there are no animals inhabiting in common the two continents, but fuch as can bear the colds of the North. Thus there are no elephants, no lions, no tigers, no camels in America; but bears, wolves, deer, and elks in abundance, abfolutely the fame in both hemifpheres. This hypothefis, which has been gaining ground ever fince its firft appearance in the world, is now reduced almoft to a certainty by the late difcoveries of Capt. Cook. That illuftrious, but unfortunate navigator, in his laft voyage, penetrated for a confiderable diftance into the ftrait which divides Afia from America, which is only fix leagues wide at its mouth; and therefore eafily practicable for canoes. We may now therefore conclude, that no farther enquiry will ever be made in to the general origin of the American tribes.

Yet, after all, it is far from being improbable that various nations, by fhipwreck, or otherwife, may have contributed, in fome degree, to the population of this continent. The Carthaginians, who had many fettlements on the coaft of Africa, beyond the Straits of Gibraltar, and pufhed their difcoveries as far as where the two continents in
that

that quarter approach each other the neareft, may probably have been thrown by tempefts on the American coaft, and the companies of the veffels finding it impracticable to return, may have incorporated with the former inhabitants, or have formed new fettlements, which, from want of the neceffary inftruments to exercife the arts they were acquainted with, would naturally degenerate into barbarity. There are indeed fome ancient writers, who give us reafon to fuppofe, that there were colonies regularly formed by that nation in America, and that the communication, after having continued for fome time, was ftopped by order of the State. But it is difficult to conceive that any people, eftablifhed with all thofe neceffaries proper for their fituation, fhould ever degenerate, from fo high a degree of cultivation as the Carthaginians poffeffed, to a total ignorance even of the moft neceffary arts : And therefore it feems probable, that if that nation ever had fuch colonies, they muft have been cut off by the natives, and every veftige of them deftroyed.

About the ninth and tenth centuries, the Danes were the greateft navigators in the univerfe. They difcovered and fettled Iceland ; and from thence, in 964, planted a colony in Greenland. The ancient Icelandic chronicles, as reported by M. Mallet, contain an account of fome Icelanders, who,

who, in the close of an unsuccessful war, fled to
Greenland, and from thence Westward, to a
country covered with vines, which from thence
they called Vinland.

The adventurers returned home, and conducted a colony to their new discovery; but disturb-
ances arising in Denmark, all communication
with Greenland, as well as Vinland, ceased; and
those countries remained unknown to the rest
of the world for several ages. The remains of
this colony are probably to be found on the coast
of Labrador, in the nation of the Esquimaux. The
colour of their skins, their hairy bodies and
bushy beards, not to mention the difference of
manners, mark an origin totally distinct from
that of the other Indians.

In the year 1170, Madoc, son of Owen Gwyn-
nedh, Prince of Wales, dissatisfied with the situation of affairs at home, left his country, as
related by the Welsh historians, in quest of new
settlements, and leaving Ireland to the North,
proceeded West till he discovered a fertile country; where, leaving a colony, he returned, and
persuading many of his country-men to join him,
put to sea with ten ships, and was never more
heard of.

This

This account has, at several times, drawn the attention of the world; but as no vestiges of them had then been found, it was concluded, perhaps too rashly, to be a fable, or at least, that no remains of the colony existed. Of late years, however, the Western settlers have received frequent accounts of a nation, inhabiting at a great distance up the Missouri, in manners and appearance resembling the other Indians, but speaking Welsh, and retaining some ceremonies of the christian worship; and at length, this is universally believed there to be a fact.

Captain Abraham Chaplain, of Kentucke, a gentleman, whose veracity may be entirely depended upon, assured the author, that in the late war, being with his company in garrison at Kaskasky, some Indians came there, and, speaking in the Welsh dialect, were perfectly understood and conversed with by two Welshmen in his company, and that they informed them of the situation of their nation as mentioned above.

The author is sensible of the ridicule which the vain and the petulant may attempt to throw on this account; but as truth only has guided his pen, he is regardless of the consequences, and flatters himself, that, by calling the attention of mankind once more to this subject, he may be the means of procuring a more accurate inquiry
into

into its truth, which, if it fhould even refute
the ftory of the Welfh, will at leaft perform the
important fervice to the world, of promoting a
more accurate difcovery of this immenfe continent.

There are feveral ancient remains in Kentucke,
which feem to prove, that this country was formerly inhabited by a nation farther advanced in
the arts of life than the Indians. Thefe are there
ufually attributed to the Welfh, who are fuppof-
ed to have formerly inhabited here; but having
been expelled by the natives, were forced to take
refuge near the fources of the Miflouri.

It is well known, that no Indian nation has e-
ver practifed the method of defending themfelves
by entrenchments; and fuch a work would even
be no eafy one, while thefe nations were unac-
quainted with the ufe of iron.

In the neighbourhood of Lexington, the remains of two ancient fortifications are to be feen,
furnifhed with ditches and baftions. One of
thefe contains about fix acres of land, and the o-
ther nearly three. They are now overgrown with
trees, which, by the number of circles in the
wood, appear to be not lefs than one hundred
and fixty years old. Pieces of earthen veffels
have alfo been plowed up near Lexington, a ma-

N   nufacture

nufacture with which the Indians were never acquainted.

The burying-grounds, which were mentioned above, under the head of Curiofities, form another ftrong argument that this country was formerly inhabited by a people different from the prefent Indians. Although they do not difcover any marks of extraordinary art in the ftructure, yet, as many nations are particularly tenacious of their ancient cuftoms, it may perhaps be worthy of enquiry, whether thefe repofitories of the dead do not bear a confiderable refemblance to the ancient Britifh remains. Some buildings, attributed to the Picts, are mentioned by the Scottifh antiquaries, which, if the author miftakes not, are formed nearly in the fame manner. Let it be enough for him to point out the road, and hazard fome uncertain conjectures. The day is not far diftant, when the fartheft recefles of this continent will be explored, and the accounts of the Welfh eftablifhed beyond the poffibility of a doubt, or configned to that oblivion which has already received fo many fuppofitions founded on arguments as plaufible as thefe.

PERSONS and HABITS.

THE Indians are not born white; and take
a great

a great deal of pains to darken their complexion, by anointing themſelves with greaſe, and lying in the ſun. They alſo paint their faces, breaſts and ſhoulders, of various colours, but generally red; and their features are well formed, eſpecially thoſe of the women. They are of a middle ſtature, their limbs clean and ſtraight, and ſcarcely any crooked or deformed perſon is to be found among them. In many parts of their bodies they prick in gun-powder in very pretty figures. They ſhave, or pluck the hair off their heads, except a patch about the crown, which is ornamented with beautiful feathers, beads, wampum, and ſuch like baubles. Their ears are pared, and ſtretched in a thong down to their ſhoulders. They are wound round with wire to expand them, and adorned with ſilver pendants, rings, and bells, which they likewiſe wear in their noſes. Some of them will have a large feather through the cartilage of the noſe; and thoſe who can afford it, wear a collar of wampum, a ſilver breaſtplate, and bracelets, on the arms and wriſts. A bit of cloth about the middle, a ſhirt of the Engliſh make, on which they beſtow innumerable broaches to adorn it, a ſort of cloth boots and mockaſons, which are ſhoes of a make peculiar to the Indians, ornamented with porcupine quills, with a blanket or match-coat thrown over all, compleats their dreſs at home; but when they go to war, they leave their trinkets behind, and

mere

mere neceffaries ferve them. There is little difference between the drefs of the men and women, excepting that a fhort petticoat, and the
hair, which is exceeding black, and long, club-
bed behind, diftinguifh fome of the latter. Except the head and eye-brows, they pluck the hair,
with great diligence, from all parts of the body,
efpecially the loofer part of the fex.

Their warlike arms are guns, bows and arrows,
darts, fcalping-knives and tomahawks. This is
one of their moft ufeful pieces of field-furni-
ture, ferving all the offices of the hatchet, pipe,
and fword. They are exceeding expert in throw-
ing it, and will kill at a confiderable diftance. The
world has no better marks-men, with any wea-
pon. They will kill birds flying, fifhes fwimming,
and wild beafts running.

G E N I U S.

T H E Indians are not fo ignorant as fome
fuppofe them, but are a very underftanding people, quick of apprehenfion, fudden in execu-
tion, fubtle in bufinefs, exquifite in invention,
and induftrious in action. They are of a very gentle and amiable difpofition to thofe they think
their friends, but as implacable in their enmity;
their revenge being only compleated, in the entire

tire deſtruction of their enemies. They are very hardy, bearing heat, cold, hunger and thirſt, in a ſurpriſing manner, and yet no people are more addicted to exceſs in eating and drinking, when it is conveniently in their power. The follies, nay miſchief, they commit when inebriated, are entirely laid to the liquor, and no one will revenge any injury (murder excepted) received from one who is no more himſelf. Among the Indians, all men are equal, perſonal qualities being moſt eſteemed. No diſtinction of birth, no rank, renders any man capable of doing pre-judice to the rights of private perſons; and there is no pre-eminence from merit, which begets pride, and which makes others too ſenſible of their own inferiority. Though there is perhaps leſs delicacy of ſentiment in the Indians than a-mongſt us; there is, however, abundantly more probity, with infinitely leſs ceremony, or equivocal compliments. Their public conferences ſhew them to be men of genius; and they have, in a high degree, the talent of natural eloquence.

They live diſperſed in ſmall villages, either in the woods, or on the banks of rivers, where they have little plantations of Indian-corn, and roots, not enough to ſupply their families half the year, and ſubſiſting the remainder of it by hunting, fiſhing and fowling, and the fruits of
the

the earth, which grow fpontaneoufly in great plenty.

Their huts are generally built of fmall logs, and covered with bark, each one having a chimney, and a door, on which they place a padlock.

Old Chelicothe is built in form of a Kentucke ftation, that is, a parallelogram, or long fquare; and fome of their houfes are fhingled A long Council-houfe extends the whole length of the town, where the King and Chiefs of the nation frequently meet, and confult of all matters of importance, whether of a civil or military nature.

Some huts are built by fetting up a frame on forks, and placing bark againft it; others of reeds, and furrounded with clay. The fire is in the middle of the wigwam, and the fmoke paffes through a little hole. They join reeds together by cords run through them, which ferve them for tables and beds. They moftly lie upon fkins of wild beafts, and fit on the ground. They have brafs kettles and pots to boil their food; gourds or calabafhes, cut afunder, ferve them for pails, cups and difhes.

RELIGION.

RELIGION.

THE accounts of travellers, concerning their religion, are various; and although it cannot be abfolutely affirmed that they have none, yet it muft be confeffed very difficult to define what it is. All agree that they acknowledge one Supreme God, but do not adore him. They have not feen him, they do not know him, believing him to be too far exalted above them, and too happy in himfelf to be concerned about the trifling affairs of poor mortals. They feem alfo to believe in a future ftate, and that after death they fhall be removed to their friends who have gone before them, to an elyfium, or paradife.

The Wyandotts, near Detroit, and fome others, have the Roman Catholic religion introduced amongft them by miffionaries. Thefe have a church, a minifter, and a regular burying-ground. Many of them appear zealous, and fay prayers in their families. Thefe, by acquaintance with white people, are a little civilized, which muft of neceffity precede chriftianity.

The Shawanefe, Cherokees, Chickafaws, and fome others, are little concerned about fuperftition, or religion. Others continue their former fuperftitious worfhip of the objects of their love
and

and fear, and especially those beings whom they
moſt dread, and whom therefore we generally de-
nominate devils; though, at the ſame time, it
is allowed they pray to the ſun, and other inferior benevolent deities, for ſucceſs in their under-
takings, for plenty of food, and other neceſſa-
ries in life.

They have their feſtivals, and other rejoicing-
days, on which they ſing and dance in a ring,
taking hands, having ſo painted and diſguiſed
themſelves, that it is difficult to know any of
them ; and after enjoying this diverſion for a
while, they retire to the place where they have
prepared a feaſt of fiſh, fleſh, fowls and fruits;
to which all are invited, and entertained with
their country ſongs. They believe that there is
great virtue in feaſts for the ſick. For this pur-
poſe a young buck muſt be killed, and boiled,
the friends and near neighbours of the patient
invited, and having firſt thrown tobacco on the
the fire, and covered it up cloſe, they all ſit down
in a ring, and raiſe a lamentable cry. They then
uncover the fire, and kindle it up ; and the head
of the buck is firſt ſent about, every one taking
a bit, and giving a loud croak, in imitation of
crows. They afterwards proceed to eat all the
buck, making a moſt harmonious, melancholy
ſong ; in which ſtrain their muſic is particularly
excellent.

As

As they approach their towns, when fome of their people are loft in war, they make great lamentations for their dead, and bear them long after in remembrance.

Some nations abhor adultery, do not approve of a plurality of wives, and are not guilty of theft; but there are other tribes that are not fo fcrupulous in thefe matters. Amongft the Chickafaws a hufband may cut off the nofe of his wife, if guilty of adultery; but men are allowed greater liberty. This nation defpifes a thief. Among the Cherokees they cut off the nofe and ears of an adulterefs; afterwards her hufband gives her a difcharge; and from this time fhe is not permitted to refufe any one who prefents himfelf. Fornication is unnoticed; for they allow perfons in a fingle ftate unbounded freedom.

Their form of marriage is fhort—the man, before witneffes, gives the bride a deer's foot, and fhe, in return, prefents him with an ear of corn, as emblems of their feveral duties.

The women are very flaves to the men; which is a common cafe in rude, unpolifhed nations, throughout the world. They are charged with being revengeful; but this revenge is only doing themfelves juftice on thofe who injure them,

O and

and is feldom executed, but in cafes of murder and adultery.

Their king has no power to put any one to death by his own authority; but the murderer is generally delivered up to the friends of the deceafed, to do as they pleafe. When one kills another, his friend kills him, and fo they continue until much blood is fhed; and at laft, the quarrel is ended by mutual prefents. Their kings are hereditary, but their authority extremely limited. No people are a more ftriking evidence of the miferies of mankind in the want of government than they. Every chief, when offended, breaks off with a party, fettles at fome diftance, and then commences hoftilities againft his own people. They are generally at war with each other. Thefe are common circumftances amongft the Indians.

When they take captives in war, they are exceedingly cruel, treating the unhappy prifoners in fuch a manner, that death would be preferable to life. They afterwards give them plenty of food, load them with burdens, and when they arrive at their towns, they muft run the gauntlet. In this, the favages exercife fo much cruelty, that one would think it impoffible they fhould furvive their fufferings. Many are killed; but if one outlives this trial, he is adopted into a family as a
son,

fon, and treated with paternal kindnefs ; and if
he avoids their fufpicions of going away, is allowed the fame privileges as their own people.

The CONCLUSION.

HAVING finifhed my intended narrative,
I fhall clofe the appendix, with a few obfervations
upon the happy circumftances, that the inhabitants of Kentucke will probably enjoy, from the
poffeffion of a country fo extenfive and fertile.

There are four natural qualities neceffary to
promote the happinefs of a country, viz. A good
foil, air, water and trade. Thefe taken collectively, excepting the latter, Kentucke poffeffes
in a fuperior degree : And, agreeable to our defcription of the weftern trade, we conclude, that
it will be nearly equal to any other on the continent of America, and the difadvantages it is fubject to, be fully compenfated by the fertility of
the foil.

This fertile region, abounding with all the lux-
uries of nature, ftored with all the principal ma-
terials for art and induftry, inhabited by virtuous and ingenious citizens, muft univerfally
attract the attention of mankind, being fituated
in the central part of the extenfive American em-
pire,

pire, (the limits of whose ample domains, as described in the second article of the late Definitive Treaty, are subjoined) where agriculture, industry, laws, arts and sciences, flourish; where afflicted humanity raises her drooping head; where springs a harvest for the poor; where conscience ceases to be a slave, and laws are no more than the security of happiness; where nature makes reparation for having created man; and government, so long prostituted to the most criminal purposes, establishes an asylum in the wilderness for the distressed of mankind.

The recital of your happiness will call to your country all the unfortunate of the earth, who, having experienced oppression, political or religious, will there find a deliverance from their chains. To you innumerable multitudes will emigrate from the hateful regions of despotism and tyranny; and you will surely welcome them as friends, as brothers; you will welcome them to partake with you of your happiness.—Let the memory of Lycurgus, the Spartan legislator, who banished covetousness, and the love of gold from his country; the excellent Locke, who first taught the doctrine of toleration; the venerable Penn, the first who founded a city of brethren; and Washington, the defender and protector of persecuted liberty, be ever the illustrious examples of your political conduct. Avail yourselves

of

of the benefits of nature, and of the fruitful country you inhabit.

Let the iron of your mines, the wool of your
flocks, your flax and hemp, the skins of the savage animals that wander in your woods, be fa-
shioned into manufactures, and take an extraordinary value from your hands. Then will you
rival the superfluities of Europe, and know that
happiness may be found, without the commerce
so universally desired by mankind.

In your country, like the land of promise,
flowing with milk and honey, a land of brooks
of water, of fountains and depths, that spring
out of valleys and hills, a land of wheat and
barley, and all kinds of fruits, you shall eat
bread without scarceness, and not lack any thing
in it; where you are neither chilled with the
cold of capricorn, nor scorched with the burning heat of cancer ; the mildness of your air so
great, that you neither feel the effects of infec-
tious fogs, nor pestilential vapours. Thus, your
country, favoured with the smiles of heaven,
will probably be inhabited by the first people the
world ever knew.

ARTICLE

ARTICLE II. *of the late* DEFINITIVE TREATY.

AND that all difputes which might arife in future on the fubject of the boundaries of the faid United States, may be prevented, it is hereby agreed and declared, that the following are and fhall be their boundaries, viz. From the N. W. angle of Nova-Scotia, viz. that angle which is formed by a line drawn due North from the fource of St. Croix River to the Highlands, along the faid Highlands, which divide thofe rivers that empty themfelves into the river St. Lawrence, from thofe which fall into the Atlantic ocean, to the North-Wefternmoft head of Connecticut River; thence down along the middle of that river to the forty-fifth degree of North latitude; from thence by a line due Weft on faid latitude, until it ftrikes the river Iroquois, or Cataraqui; thence along the middle of the faid river into Lake Ontario, through the middle of the faid lake, until it ftrikes the communication by water between that lake and Lake Erie; thence along the middle of faid communication into Lake Erie, through the middle of faid lake until it arrives at the water communication between that lake and Lake Huron; thence along the middle of faid water communication into the Lake Huron; thence through the middle of faid lake to the water communication between that

that lake and Lake Superior; thence through Lake Superior Northward of the Isles Royal and Phelipeaux to the Long Lake; thence through the middle of said Long Lake and the water communication between it and the Lake of the Woods, to the Lake of the Woods; thence through the said lake to the most N. W. point thereof, and from thence on a due West course to the river Mississippi; thence by a line to be drawn along the middle of the said river Mississippi until it shall intersect the Northernmost part of the thirty-first degree of North latitude; South, by a line to be drawn due East from the determination of the last mentioned in the latitude of thirty-one degrees North of the equator, to the middle of the river Apalachicola, or Catanouche; thence along the middle thereof to its junction with the Flint River; thence straight to the head of St. Mary's River; and thence down along the middle of St. Mary's River to the Atlantic ocean; East, by a line to be drawn along the middle of the river St. Croix, from its mouth in the bay of Fundy to its source, and from its source directly North to the aforesaid Highlands which divide the rivers that fall into the Atlantic ocean from those which fall into the river St. Lawrence, comprehending all islands within twenty leagues of any part of the shores of the United States, and lying between lines to be drawn due East from the points where the aforesaid boundaries

between

between Nova-Scotia on the one part, and East-Florida on the other, shall respectively touch the bay of Fundy and the Atlantic ocean, excepting such islands as now are, or hertofore have been, within the limits of the said province of Nova-Scotia.

ROADS

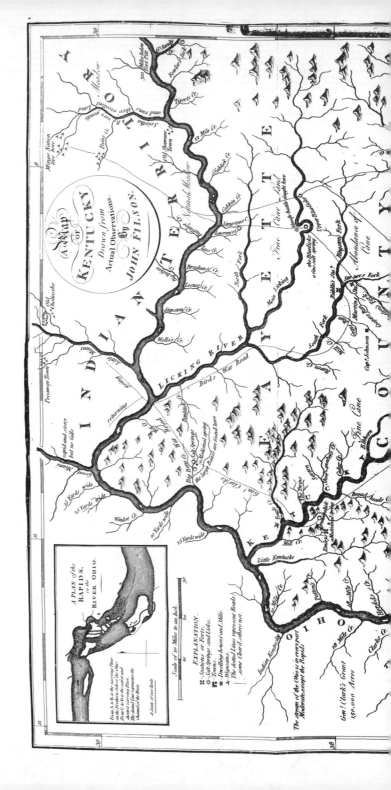

A Map of KENTUCKY Drawn from Actual Observations. By JOHN FILSON.

A PLAN of the RAPIDS in the RIVER OHIO.

From A. to B. is the carrying Place on the Northern Side of the Ohio. From C. to D. is the worst and shortest carrying Place. The dotted Line represents the Channel of the River.

A Scale of two Rods.

EXPLANATION.
H — Stations or Forts.
O — Salt Springs and Licks.
⊞ — Towns.
▲ — Dwelling houses and Mills.
⚷ — Wigwams.
— — The abbreviated Lines represent Roads Course Cleared, others not.

Scale of 10 Miles to an Inch.

The stream of the Ohio is in every part Moderate, except the Rapids.

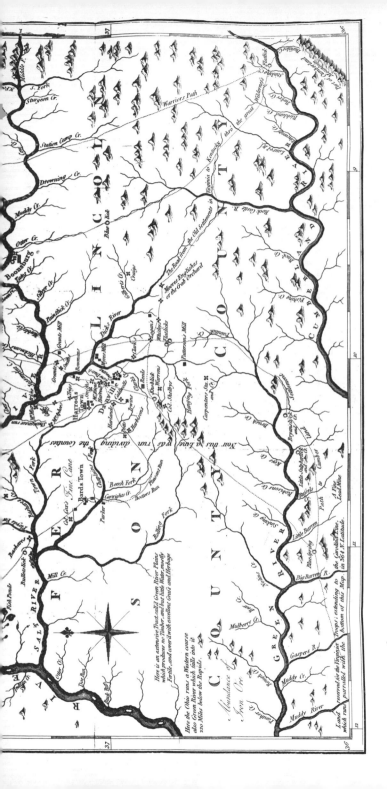

R O A D from Philadelpia to the Falls of the Ohio by land.

	M	M.D
FROM Philadelphia to Lancaster	66	
To Wright's on Sufquehannah	10	76
To York-town	12	88
Abbott's-town	15	103
Hunter's-town	10	113
the mountain at Black's Gap	3	116
the other fide of the mountain	7	123
the Stone-houfe Tavern	25	148
Wadkin's Ferry on Potowmack	14	162
Martinfburg	13	175
Winchefter	20	195
Newtown	8	203
Stover's-town	10	213
Woodftock	12	225
Shanandoah River	15	240
the North branch of Shanandoah	29	269
Stanton	15	284
the North Fork of James River	37	321
James River	18	339
Botetourt Court-houfe	12	351
Woods's on Catauba River	21	372
Patterfon's on Roanoak	9	381
the Allegany Mountain	8	389
New River	12	401
the forks of the road	16	417

P   To

	M	M. D
To Fort Chiffel - -	12	429
a Stone Mill - -	11	440
Boyd's - - -	8	448
head of Holftein - -	5	453
Wafhington Court-houfe -	45	498
the Block-houfe - - -	35	533
Powel's Mountain - -	33	566
Walden's Ridge - - -	3	569
the Valley Station - -	4	573
Martin Cabbin's - -	25	598
Cumberland Mountain -	20	618
the ford of Cumberland River	13	631
the Flat Lick - -	9	640
Stinking Creek - -	2	642
Richland Creek - -	7	649
Down Richland Creek - -	8	657
Rackoon Spring - -	6	663
Laurel River - -	2	665
Hazle Patch - - -	15	680
the ford on Rock-Caftle River	10	690
Englifh's Station - -	25	715
Col. Edwards's at Crab-Orchard	3	718
Whitley's Station - -	5	723
Logan's Station - -	5	728
Clark's Station - -	7	735
Crow's Station - -	4	739
Harrod's Station - -	3	742
Harland's - -	4	746
		To

	M	M.D
To Harbison's – –	10	756
Bard's-town – –	25	781
the Salt-works – –	25	806
the Falls of the Ohio –	20	826

Kentucke is situated about South, 60° West from Philadelphia, and, on a straight line, may be about six hundred miles distant from that city.

———————————————————

ROAD to Pittsburg, and Distances from thence down the Ohio River to its mouth, and from thence down the Mississippi to the Mexican Gulph.

	M	M.D
FROM Philadelphia to Lancaster	66	
To Middletown – –	26	92
Harris's Ferry –	10	102
Carlisle – –	17	119
Shippensburgh – –	21	140
Chamber's-town –	11	151
Fort Loudon – –	13	164
Fort Littleton – –	18	182
Juniata Creek – –	19	201

To

	M	M.D
To Bedford - -	14	215
the foot of the Allegany Mountains	15	230
Stony-Creek - - -	15	245
the East side of Laurel Hill	12	257
Fort Ligonier - -	9	266
Pittsburg -	54	320

FROM Pittsburg to Log's-town on the Ohio River, N. side,	18	
To Big Beaver-Creek, N. -	11	29
Little Beaver-Creek, N. -	13	42
Yellow-Creek, N. -	9	51
Ming's Town - -	18	69
Grass-Creek, N. - -	2	71
Wheelen-Creek, S. side, -	25	96
Grave-Creek, S. -	10	106
the Long-Reach - -	16	122
the end of do. - -	15	137
Miskingum River, N. -	23	160
Little Kenhawa, S. -	12	172
Hockhocking River, N. -	13	185
Great Kenhawa River, S. -	11	196
Great Griandot, S. -	24	220
Big Sandy-Creek, S. -	13	233
Sciotha River, N. -	45	278
Big Buffalo-Lick Creek, S.	24	302
a Large Island -	20	322
the Three Islands -	10	332
Limestone-Creek, S. -	7	339
Little Miami, N. -	65	404

To

	M.	M.D.
To Licking River, South fide,	8	412
Great Miami River, N.	27	439
Big-Bone Creek, S.	32	471
Kentucke River, S.	44	515
the Rapids of Ohio	77	592
Salt River, S.	23	615
the beginning of the Low Country	132	747
the firft of the Five Iflands	38	785
Green River, S.	27	812
a Large Ifland	58	870
Wabafh River, N.	40	910
the Great Cave, N.	62	972
Cumberland River, S.	33	1005
Tenefe River, S.	12	1017
Fort Meffia-River, S.	11	1028
the mouth of Ohio River	46	1074
the Iron Banks, S.	15	1089
Chickafaw River	67	1156
the River Margot	104	1160
St. Francis's River	70	1230
Akanfa River	108	1338
Yazaw River	165	1503
the Grand Gulph	39	1542
the Little Gulph	14	1556
Fort Rofalie, at the Natches,	31	1587
the River Rouge	36	1643
the uppermoft mouth of the Miffiffippi	3	1646

To

	M.	M.D.
To Point Coupée -	50	1696
Ibberville - -	35	1731
the Villages of the Alibama } Indians -	39	1770
New Orleans, S. fide, -	60	1830
the mouths of the Miffiffippi	105	1935

A ftraight line drawn from Pittfburg to the mouth of the Miffiffippi may be computed at two thirds of the diftance by the meanders of the rivers, which will be twelve hundred and ninety miles.